Praise for *Broken Body, Healing Sp...*
Lectio Divina and Living with Illness

"Mary Earle's creative use of the spiritual practice of *lectio divina* invites readers to seek God in times of illness through a careful process of listening that resists easy answers yet offers life-giving hope. Wise and gentle, this book offers practical guidance to a generation of Christians who live at some distance from both their bodies and their souls."

—Frederick W. Schmidt, author of *When Suffering Persists*

"Through her personal struggle with debilitating illness, Mary Earle learned to listen deeply to the language of her body. This moving account, which includes the stories of others dealing with sickness, offers simple yet profound models for prayer based on the ancient Benedictine wisdom of *lectio divina*. By paying attention to physical pain and emotional stress comes the discovery of holy Presence and even joy in the experience of illness. The authenticity of this book shines through its pages to support healing and hope.

—Rev. Elizabeth Canham, author of *Heart Whispers: Benedictine Wisdom for Today*

BROKEN BODY, HEALING SPIRIT

Lectio Divina and Living with Illness

MARY C. EARLE

Morehouse Publishing
NEW YORK • HARRISBURG • DENVER

FOR MY FAMILY
and for Lesley Marcus, Marga Speicher, and Dr. Jocelynn Theard,
healers and friends

Morehouse Publishing, 4775 Linglestown Road, Harrisburg, PA 17112

Morehouse Publishing, 445 Fifth Avenue, New York, NY 10016

Morehouse Publishing is an imprint of Church Publishing Incorporated.
www.churchpublishing.org

Library of Congress Cataloging-in-Publication Data

Earle, Mary C.
   Broken body, healing spirit : lectio divina and living with illness / by Mary C. Earle.
       p. cm.
   Includes bibliographical references.
   ISBN 978-0-8192-1928-2 (pbk.)
   1. Bible--Devotional use. 2. Diseases--Religious aspects--Christianity. I. Title.
   BS617.8.E37 2003
   248.8'61--dc21   2002152800

Printed in the United States of America

Contents

∼

Jesus did not come to explain away suffering or remove it. He came to fill it with his presence.

—*Paul Claudel*

Acknowledgments

~

I am particularly grateful to Susan Hanson for her reading of the manuscript and for her good critique, and to Debra Farrington and Nancy Fitzgerald for their editorial skill. I also thank the members of the several classes I have offered on living with illness at St. Mark's Episcopal Church in San Antonio and at the Episcopal Seminary of the Southwest in Austin. Their insight, wisdom, and courage were invaluable in the crafting of this text. The Reverend Michael Chalk, rector of St. Mark's, has offered support and encouragement for the vocation of writing, a gift beyond measure. Sylvia Maddox provided the impetus for this book through her insistence that I write about what I have learned. My husband Doug has been a steadfast companion, in sickness and in health; he knew the book was ready for writing before I did.

Portions of this text appeared as an article, "Reading the Text of an Illness," in *Presence: The Journal for Spiritual Directors International*, vol. 6, no. 1, January 2000, 7–11.

A NOTE TO THE READER

If you are living with illness, be mindful of your own physical, emotional, and spiritual limitations as you read this book and engage the suggested practices of prayer. Go at your own pace. If you have questions about the appropriateness of a practice for your own condition, check with a doctor, spiritual director, or other caregiver.

CHAPTER 1

Introduction

∼

I n the summer of 1995, I had just returned from a vacation in northern California. Feeling well and relaxed from my time away, I had no idea that an attack of acute pancreatitis was about to change my life completely. The Sunday prior to the attack, I felt fine. I went about my regular duties as a parish priest. On Monday, after having breakfast and sending my husband off to work, I became violently ill, so ill that I could barely make it to the telephone. A ride in an ambulance followed, then a hospitalization. Months of snail-slow recovery ensued. Then there was yet another attack and hospitalization and even more months of recovery.

Throughout all of this I discovered what everyone who suffers from illness in its acute, chronic, or progressive forms eventually learns: being sick rudely interrupts life as you know it. Plans, hopes, dreams—everything from trips abroad to new employment to advanced college degrees to enjoyment of grandchildren—all go by the wayside. Life changes color, tone, and texture. You make the acquaintance of something that is "other," something that lives within the housing of your body. Illness forces you to inhabit a reality that our culture rejects completely, a reality marked by real limitation, physical frailty, and a variety of constraints that curtail your activities.

In the hospital following my first attack, friends, parishioners, and fellow clergy came to see me, and rare was the visitor who didn't come with an interpretation—almost all unhelpful—of my illness. My visitors offered me a variety of ways to read the text of my illness, ranging from the pseudo-Christian proclamation that "God must want you to be a saint" (sadly not said in jest) to the kind of remark that contemporary spirituality writer Joan Borysenko calls "New Age fundamentalism."[1] In my case this New Age fundamentalism looked like the literal reading of the body, equating each malady or each organ with a particular affliction of the spirit. Since my pancreas was the afflicted organ, I was told that I didn't have enough sweetness in my life, presumably because the pancreas, in its creation of insulin, regulates blood sugar levels.

At a time when I was at my most vulnerable, I found myself besieged with others' opinions and interpretations. I was surprised by the avalanche of unsolicited advice. I was overwhelmed by so many notions of the meaning of the experience of falling acutely ill. So in the long months of recovery, I began to search for a way to read my illness and my body on my own. I wanted to allow myself—and other people like me—the chance to study the narrative, or the story, of what had happened, and to bring that narrative into prayer and reflection. The quick and ready interpretations that are so often handed to someone who is ill overlook the specific reality of each person, and the particular experience of being sick and weakened.

If you've lived with illness, you know exactly what it's like when other people so readily interpret your experience. But you have the capacity, with support, to interpret it yourself, letting the experience become a sacred text, a life narrative full of meaning—even if the meaning is veiled, even if your plans are interrupted, even if you live in wrenching pain. Your body may be full of clues about what this illness means in your life, clues that shouldn't be met with formulaic responses that stop your story before it is told. The text of your illness is embedded within the text of your life—your particular life with your own particular questions, hopes, dreams, griefs, and aspirations.

READING THE TEXT

As I recovered from my attacks and pondered how to re-vision my illness and my life, I realized that one of my own prayer practices could help me. For years the practice of *lectio divina*, or sacred reading, has fed my spiritual life. Why couldn't it nourish the life and spirit of my body as well?

In the late 1970s a friend lent me audiotapes of a retreat led by the Reverend Mark Dyer, who later became the bishop of the Episcopal Diocese of Bethlehem, Pennsylvania. On those tapes, he introduced the Benedictine practice of *lectio divina*, a way of reading and praying Scripture. I clearly remember standing in the kitchen, chopping vegetables for salad while listening as he spoke of this way of praying. As I went about the ordinary activity of preparing dinner, his voice described the activity of regularly engaging Scripture with an open heart. I stood in the space so regularly inhabited by my family, and it began to dawn on me that this way of praying was intended for those who were not experts. *Lectio divina* was a way to listen to God through Scripture for someone like me, a mom with two small children. Bishop Dyer's voice, at once lighthearted and learned, hinted at the formative nature of *lectio divina*, which became a regular way of praying for me. From time to time I tried other forms, but inevitably I was drawn back to *lectio* as the basis for ongoing prayer as a way to encounter the living presence of God through Scripture.

In a fast-food culture, *lectio* invites us to the scriptural banquet, to savor the richness of what we are offered, to dally at the table. With *lectio* we read slowly and allow ourselves time to digest and absorb our spiritual food. And because it is reflective and slow, *lectio* leads us gently away from pat answers and smug conclusions. Over time, *lectio* leads us into the path of life, into a way of knowing that is marked by knowing how much we do not know. *Lectio* shapes us in such a way that we begin to perceive our lives and the contexts in which they unfold in a new way. We begin to see that the living Word is present within and through the events of our lives. *Lectio divina* invites us to read the text of our lives, to listen to what is occurring, to approach both our personal and our corporate lives with care and attention. At that point, we discover that our lives are, in fact, a scripture in and of themselves, a story that is unfolding day by day.

Though the Latin name makes it sound difficult, this practice of holy reading is not esoteric or spiritually ambitious. It's as ordinary as making a peanut butter sandwich. The practice itself has roots in the early monastic life of the Christian church, a life that began to flourish in the third and fourth centuries C.E. The Rule of St. Benedict, written in the sixth century, gives instruction for this way of reading and praying Scripture, reading and praying our lives. Benedict calls the pattern of life he offers a "little Rule for beginners."[2] With common sense and kindliness, he invites those who are not inclined to spiritual heights to begin regular practice of prayer, study, and work—inviting us not to be gurus, but beginners. We don't have to be experts in Christianity, simply practitioners who are willing to keep trying.

The invitation to be a beginner was attractive to me, and over time, the practice of *lectio divina* became an essential part of my prayer life. It also made me uncomfortable with my tendencies toward control and my aspirations to be spiritually astute. Using *lectio divina* regularly, I began to see that the locus of a Christian life was the ordinary, daily interactions of family, office, classroom, grocery store. Benedict's Rule led me gently away from the esoteric heights of spirituality, and *lectio* invited me to read life differently than I had before. No doubt arriving at midlife also deepened my distrust of certitudes. The reading of situations, contexts, world events brought more questions than answers, more wondering than dictates, more unknowing than knowing. Without being aware consciously that the shift was taking place, I began reading my life.

Surprisingly, in all of this unknowing and undoing, I began to recognize that my clear and precise theology had once again succeeded in putting God in a box as I tried to fit the irreducible forces of life and death into my clever categories. I don't intend to diminish theological reflection or careful intellectual endeavor. Both are necessary to Christian practice and are invaluable to the faithful journeys of many. But I had fallen prey to that most tempting of theological idols—the making of my theology into a god. The ordinary practice of *lectio divina* had an unexpected subversive effect. I began to be uncomfortable with my own reductionist versions of both Scripture and life itself.

Lectio divina with Scripture, *lectio divina* with life, delivered me from my own little idolatries. Fresh air began blowing within my heart and soul again, hinting at what Mother Teresa of Calcutta, the Roman Catholic nun who served the poor and dying, meant when she spoke of "Christ in his distressing disguises."[3] As I read my life as a text, I began to experience more silence than chatter, more awe than explanation. My identities as daughter, mother, sister, wife, priest began to be woven together—not through any spectacular means, but simply through paying attention to the ordinary connections and points of contact. I began to get the gist of what Benedictine sister and spirituality writer Joan Chittister meant when she wrote, "Daily life is the stuff of which high sanctity can be made."[4] The text we are called to pray, read, mark, learn, and inwardly digest is the living scripture of God in Christ indwelling our common daily lives.

OUR FEARS OF ILLNESS AND MORTALITY

My interest in finding a new way to understand and live with illness is not only personal, but professional. As a parish priest I spend a lot of time offering spiritual direction to others who live with illness, and I hear many stories that are very much like mine. Those who are ill are often on the receiving end of boundless advice on how to think and feel about their experience. While often well intended, the advice has the effect of obscuring or covering over the feelings of the person who is ill. The unsolicited counsel tends to have an anxious edge to it or a "fix-it" tone.

Why this rush to interpret illness and offer advice? Maybe this need to pinpoint the meaning of illness speaks volumes about our unease with the fact that we can weaken and die.

Within Christian circles especially, there may be a strange anxiety when sick people aren't cured: maybe they just don't have enough faith, or pray enough, or trust enough. But implicit assumptions about cause and effect are sadly simplistic. There is nothing quite as destructive to a person living with chronic illness as the kind of remark that usually takes this form: "We are praying so hard for you. We just cannot figure out why you don't get well." The implication is that somehow the person living with the ailment is at fault. It's Job's friends in twenty-first-century clothing, still looking for fault, still blaming the victim. They are often afraid to embrace the reality of God suffering with us.

Labeling can be punitive, too. For the person who lives with illness, it can create even more disconnection, isolation, and alienation than the illness itself does. A woman with breast cancer is told, "You don't value yourself as a woman, or you wouldn't have this particular cancer." Parents with an adult child suffering from an intractable epileptic disorder are told, "Pray more, have more faith." A young man struggling to come to terms with his new diagnosis of being bipolar is advised, "Just go to the local healing service and everything will be fine." But pronouncements like these ignore the particularity of each life. While many people live daily with some form of illness, each person does it differently. Some are coming to know their lives within the context of a new chronic disorder. Others are living with the steady eroding of physical ability of a progressive ailment. Yet others are seeking to find meaning and life within the harrowing pattern of chemotherapy and radiation. Each person, each illness, is a particular story—a story told through a particular person in his own context, in her own time and place. Each story is full of sacred meaning. Discerning the meaning, listening for intimations of divine presence in the

midst of confusion, disorientation, and pain requires what the
Benedictine tradition calls "listening with the ear of the heart."

The listening begins by jettisoning pat interpretations. As
you practice this way of listening and discerning, you will need
to learn patience. And more often than not, you will need the
companionship of a friend, spiritual director, or a group of fellow travelers in the land of illness. This kind of listening allows
the text of the illness to unfold, often slowly. Just as illness
causes us to reexamine our identities, so too illness will directly
affect our prayer. With *lectio divina* as a guide, the spiritual life
of one who is ill begins to be reshaped. The irreducible, imme-
diate presence of God revealed in and through the suffering, in
and through the *lectio divina*, upends old patterns. Something
new begins to take form from the ground up. The body that is
broken becomes the locus for a spiritual life that is grounded in
the everyday reality of living with illness. This book offers a way
of engaging in the spiritual practice of *lectio divina* as one listens to the text of a body that is ill, of a life that is afflicted.

LISTENING TO THE BODY

The idea of listening to the body may seem strange at first. In
Western culture some of us are so divorced from our own flesh
that we tend to live as if we are pure spirit, disconnected from
bone, tissue, lymph, and marrow. Others work on sculpting
their bodies, trying to force them into an idealized image of
perfection. Fitness is a laudable quest, but it might be a good
idea to ask ourselves why we are so consumed with needing a
perfect body. Am I so disgusted with my body that I try to force
it to "shape up"? Or do I want to support this intricate system
of organs in which I live and move and have my being? Could
it be that I am invited to embrace the proclamation that each

human person is a place "wherein the Holy Spirit makes a dwelling"?[5]

Illness, in a peculiar way, confronts us with what the early church termed the "scandal of the Incarnation."[6] As we read about our particular affliction, we may come to realize that some power is at work in our very flesh and bones, creating, redeeming, and sanctifying on the most intimate submolecular level. We may find ourselves pondering the fact that a body that has been overwhelmed by illness is also a body wherein life dwells. Disruptive, distressing, and acutely confusing, illness calls us to a deepening awareness of the wonder of the body, an awareness that we did not bring ourselves into being, and that it is through our embodied life that we encounter the presence of the God in whom we live and move and have our being.

We may begin to be aware of the mysterious, hidden workings that happen within our flesh. Or we awaken abruptly to the fact that respiration, circulation, digestion, all occur without our conscious intervention. Through illness, the embodied nature of our lives grabs our attention, and forces us to befriend the very flesh we thought betrayed us. The body that we had taken for granted turns out to be a rich and varied text, full of layers of meaning and symbol. Those who are Christians are faced with the terrible irony that we who proclaim the Incarnation of the Word made flesh have failed to perceive the living Word within us, within our own cells and organs. The Christ "in [whom] all things hold together" (Col 1:17) holds together each atom, each molecule, each cell, each organ, each body. Were that not the case, there would be no bodies. There would be no persons.

Beginning to read the body, to tend the body, ultimately confronts us with the intimate presence of this Christ in whom all things hold together. We are led to realize that we did not bring ourselves into being, and that on any given day, outside of eating and sleeping, our bodily activities go on without conscious care and attention. Yet the body that houses our souls, in which our embodied identity and personhood abide, is continually in the process of being made new. Daily, nutrients and oxygen are used to make new cells. Old cells die and are excreted. Through no conscious participation on our part, the process of dying and rising continues on a cellular level.

READING THE TEXT OF AN ILLNESS: AN EXAMPLE

To give you an idea of what I mean, here's the story of someone whose experience became a meaningful text for her. (The stories in this book are being used with permission, though I've changed the names.) Alice's illness required weekly blood tests for some months, and she began to dread them. Her veins were hard to find and she encountered the moment of "just a little stick" with great trepidation. Inevitably the technician would miss the vein, and things would go from bad to worse.

One day, her arm blue and purple from her latest test, Alice visited a friend who was in cancer treatment. He rolled up his sleeve to show her his own purpled arm. At that moment, Alice realized she was part of a community, a hidden community of those who have difficulty with blood tests. That small moment made a big difference in her life. Her arm and her friend's arm bore something that looked like tribal markings. They bore the signs, in their flesh, of the ongoing wounding that allowed them to continue living.

Alice discovered that other people's experiences with blood tests could help her with her own. A nurse told her that getting nervous increased her adrenalin, which made the veins shrink even more. The realization that her very blood vessels were shrinking from being poked helped Alice see the humorous side of the situation. Her own anxiety was one of the problems, and she could do something to control that. As she remembered her friend's rolled-up sleeve and wounded arm, her prayer became "By our wounds we are healed." She needed the blood tests to maintain some degree of health, and she began to see those tests, and the wounding they caused, as a form of healing, a necessary part of her own participation in the process of living with her illness. She also began to speak up, to tell the technicians that she had especially small veins that a well-practiced technician would handle easily. She saw herself as a partner with Christ in the process of healing that these tests brought about.

For Alice, the first step to living well with her illness was taking the time to pay attention to her experience and reading the text of her purple arm. Then she began to reflect on that experience. In her prayers she held the image of her friend's wounded arm alongside her own. She learned to listen deeply to the image. She sketched the two arms in her journal, using colors to draw in the veins and the bruising. In so doing, she started learning to live with the illness and its treatment in a new way. Outwardly, not much changed. Alice still had to have the regular tests. But she had a different way of reading her own experience and using that knowledge to live more fully.

BEGINNING AGAIN

In the chapters that follow, I want to apply the historic practice of *lectio divina* in a practical way and give you some suggestions for reflection and prayer. *Lectio divina* applied in this way helps you, as you live with illness, to listen to the Word that is speaking through the context of your life, through the grind of blood work and diagnostic tests, and the jolting experience of having your body cut open and your organs handled. Learning to read the text of the illness this way doesn't provide any magical cures. But it does give you a way to perceive Presence within the illness and to discover community in the process.

This practice is not the only way to pray through—and learn to live with—an illness. It's just one way, one approach that has helped some people. And it's not primarily a theological reflection, though incarnational theology is its clear underpinning and foundation. As Christians, we proclaim that "the Word became flesh and lived among us" (John 1:14). That is my starting point in reflecting on the body, on illness, on life, and on faith. St. Benedict's "little Rule for beginners" invites us all to approach our lives with an open mind and an open heart. For those who live with illness, even when—especially when—sadness, grief, anger, and confusion mark our inner hearts, the Rule offers transforming medicine. Living with illness is never easy. But Benedict's gentleness offers those who travel with illness an opportunity to begin a relationship with the afflicted flesh, an open-ended relationship that offers a path of life even as we go down to the grave saying, "Alleluia, alleluia!"

A WORD FOR FAMILIES, FRIENDS, CAREGIVERS OF THOSE LIVING WITH ILLNESS

This book is directed to the persons living with illness. However, illness affects families and friends as well as those who are ill. Much of what follows may be adapted to your own experience of living with a person who is ill. Taking the time to read your own text of living with illness may be the best gift you can give your family member or friend. As you become acquainted with your own worries, pressures, anxieties, fears, hopes, and discoveries, you will be more open to hearing and perceiving what is happening for you, as well as what is happening for your loved one who is ill.

Living with someone who is chronically or progressively ill can cause real disruption and stress for a family. Those who find themselves in this position are invited to read this book with the awareness that their own lives—even if they're healthy—are altered by illness. The practices offered at the end of the chapters can be adapted to your own needs and experiences. Simply begin by reading your own text, by paying attention to your own perspectives and impressions. Allow yourself to recognize your own suffering and distress, and to hear the story being told within that context.

You may discover that your own body, in the stress of being a caregiver, is asking for care and attention. Allowing yourself time and space to tend your own experience in the light of the gospel will help you to live faithfully within the difficult, sometimes conflicted, circumstances of being with a loved one who is ill.

CHAPTER 2

The Practice of *Lectio Divina*

~

INTRODUCTION

M any years ago, when I first took ballet lessons, we spent much time on the basic positions. Everything flowed from those simple embodied patterns. Every lesson began with the instructor gently checking the alignment of my head, spine, and feet. Very gently, she would place her hand on my hip or back, letting my body get the feel of the position. Over time, it took less and less concentration to stand in the position. My body knew what the pattern was. Thanks to the guidance of Mrs. Matlock, I could find the position. Thanks to her particular kindness, which allowed for the idiosyncrasies of each little body, there was a joy in stepping into the position.

he same is true with a rule of life, which gives attention to body, mind, and spirit. Although there are a variety of rules, just as there are varieties of people, all include regular prayer, relationships, Scripture, daily living, rest, and labor—these are the raw material to which a rule gives shape.

We receive the tradition of *lectio divina* from the Rule of Saint Benedict of Nursia, a sixth-century monk who came from a town in central Italy. Benedict's Rule continues to be the pattern for monastic communities in the Anglican, Roman Catholic, and Lutheran traditions. Establishing guidelines for living out the faith, Benedict's Rule, rather than binding those who adhere to it, offers a simple pattern for living organized around three basic orientations: prayer, study, and manual labor or work.

Lectio divina, or holy reading, is an essential part of the Benedictine rhythm. The Rule itself seems to be the fruit of *lectio,* for the Rule creates a communal space in which conversation is encompassed by silence. Within each person, within communal interaction, hurry and haste are put aside as we're invited to become aware of our frenetic way of life, and to slow down and really listen. The practice of *lectio divina,* this savoring of Scripture and of life itself, permits a kind of encounter that leads to pondering. We encounter the text and are encountered by the text. In that meeting something new and fresh opens up, bringing together the microcosm of our own experience and the macrocosm of the received sacred text. Though I might read the same psalm every morning, because I bring new experience to the text each day, the potential for wider and deeper understanding is always there.

There is an organic dimension to *lectio,* for readers intentionally bring their own lives to the text. The encounter between text and reader happens in an open space of listening, a space in which the memory, reason, and skills of our lives meet the Word found indwelling the text. This is a mutual indwelling, for Christ indwells us and we indwell Christ—the lived experience described in Jesus' words from the Gospel of John: "As you, Father, are in me and I am in you, may they also be in us" (John 17:21). The practitioner of *lectio* comes to the text expecting to be addressed, to be known, to be met.

Lectio divina is also a dynamic practice. Though the basic pattern of *lectio* remains the same, the life experience that we bring to the text changes from day to day. And, by following a lectionary, the text will change from day to day, too. An ongoing conversation marked by deep listening begins to unfold, a conversation between ourselves and the living Presence whom we encounter through this meditative approach to Scripture. Scripture speaks to our lives; our lives speak to the text. This daily conversation focuses our attention, informs our living, and leads us out of cramped little closets of devotional rigidity.

As our experience of Scripture becomes more organic and dynamic, the practice of *lectio divina* affects the way we interpret our lives, our histories, our memories, our illnesses. *Lectio* provokes questions about our tendencies to reduce experience to pat formulas and, as we live with illness, challenges our assumptions that our experience can be handled by simple labels and interpretations. We begin to notice our own discomfort with facile readings of our bodies' travail. We allow our own questions, desires, fears, confusions, and uncertainties to rise to the surface. Underneath this movement is a growing trust that the stress and chaos of the illness may have within it the seeds of new creation. Over time we find that something is tugging on our awareness, and that something is the possibility that in all of this loss there may eventually be signs of life.

Writing from a time and place far removed from the twenty-first century, Benedict sets out a pattern that is balanced and humane even for today. The Rule stands as a challenge to our assumption that we have to hurry, that we have to make quick decisions and fast readings. It encourages us to pay attention to the beginning and ending of each day, and to the turning of the seasons as we perceive life within the larger context of creation, a cosmos designed by divine delight and intent. Within this larger context, small details are noted and cherished—the handling of the utensils of the kitchen, the greeting of guests, the amount of wine served with meals—and daily life becomes the sacred space in which divine and human encounter transpires continually. We are invited to live out the union already accomplished through the mystery and grace of the Incarnation.

If you've been ill, you know what it's like when your body forces you to slow down or stop altogether. But even though you'd rather keep going, the slower pace allows you to notice your own unease with a superficial reading of the text of your life. The slowing allows your wondering, your questions, your anxiety, your hope to make themselves known. When illness causes you to enter stillness and solitude, you may at first be anxious or uneasy. But in time, that very stillness and solitude will offer the opportunity to reflect on your life and how you're called to live it.

THE PROCESS OF *LECTIO DIVINA*

Benedict's Rule offers a way of reading Scripture based on five stages: silence *(silencio)*, reading *(lectio)*, meditating *(meditatio)*, praying *(oratio)*, and contemplating *(contemplatio)*. While the practice suggests a way to "read, mark, learn and inwardly digest"[7] the scriptural text, there's also a wider application. The practice allows us to read our lives in this way, as we reflect on our events, relationships, dreams, and experiences to find the presence of Christ in the midst of our lives. *Lectio* invites us to reflect regularly on all that we live through and live with, and to be on the alert for meaning and direction even in the midst of diagnostic tests, hospitalizations, blood work, CAT scans, and endless visits to the doctor. It shows a way of approaching that "text" of illness—and the the text of Scripture—with an openness of heart, soul, and mind. This is an openness that allows the Spirit of God to illumine the darkness—even when, from our perspective, the darkness remains dark, when the illness progresses, when severe weakness causes disorientation. Let's apply the pattern of *lectio divina* reading a psalm.

Silencio

Though this book applies *lectio* to the text of illness, let's first try it as we read Scripture. First, come to a place of silence. This silence is that of hope that puts aside both the visual and aural stimuli that keep us engaged at a surface level. As you move into this stage of *silencio,* you start by stopping. Put aside noise, sit still, take the time to check in with your body. Sometimes it helps to stretch or to walk slowly, and then to note your pattern of breathing. As your flow of breath begins to call your attention and you become present to the text of Scripture and to your own listening heart, you're greeted by the silence that dwells within you, where the Spirit moves with sighs too deep for words. You discover that there is a gracious and tender Presence, waiting in silence beneath and beyond the myriad thoughts, opinions, and memories rushing to your attention. You encounter the Presence in whom all things hold together— your body, your soul, even your buzzing thoughts.

If this practice is brand new for you, don't expect an automatic shift in your awareness. As with almost anything that you hope to embrace as a character-forming habit, this kind of silence requires patience and practice. Be gentle with yourself, but be persistent, too. Don't lapse into judging each experience. *Lectio divina* isn't a contest or a self-improvement program but a way of making yourself available for an encounter with the living God— and even with yourself. As you slow down enough to notice the thoughts and feelings stirring within you, you await the moment of meeting. And when it comes, who knows what might happen?

Lectio

After engaging the silence, move to the text itself. Don't be a speed reader—after all, you're not reading for information. Instead, come to the text listening for the voice of the living God, for a word intended for this day, this moment. Come to the text knowing that the Incarnate Word will speak, through these words, directly to you. You'll have the sense that a particular word, or phrase, or verse is intended only for you.

Remember that in the early years of the church, when manuscripts were laboriously hand copied and many of the faithful were illiterate, *lectio* was accomplished not by reading, but by recalling Scripture that had been committed to memory. In a way, the Scripture called to the person, welling up from the pool of memory, tugging at the edge of awareness for attention. There is an element of recognition in the practice of *lectio*, of encountering a word or phrase and doing a double-take of the soul. Have you ever had the sense of remembering something essential you thought you'd forgotten? Have you ever seen a face in a crowd and felt it was familiar and dear? Then you understand something important about *lectio*. At the heart of remembering is the growing awareness that you are called back to your true self, your deepest self, hid with Christ.

Lectio is also ever-new. Even if you read the same passage for days on end, with each reading you bring new moments of your life into conversation with the scriptural text. Then the text that is Scripture meets the dynamic text of your life, bringing something new into being. The dynamic nature of this kind of reading can be disconcerting if you're accustomed to reading Scripture as if its meaning were always one-dimensional and clearly established. If you're used to being told what a text means, rather than discerning meaning within the context of a worshiping community, then reading life or illness and looking for layers of meaning may seem absurd. On the other hand, a version of *lectio* occurs in many Bible study groups when the participants are asked, "What does this say to you today?" The question itself implies a variety of possible interpretations.

It's also worth noting that the practice of *lectio* does not exclude the use of modern exegetical tools such as commentaries or theological word dictionaries. Indeed, these kinds of aids enhance the reading by amplifying and enriching the nuances of the text.

Meditatio

Once a word or phrase captures the attention of your heart, stop reading. Go no further. These are the words that will serve as your food for the day. In the remaining steps of *lectio,* mull them over, chewing them as a cow would chew her cud. (This is Benedict's metaphor for the slow ingestion of the Word that comes with listening and reading in this way.) Chew the words slowly, seeking nourishment and savoring their flavor on your spiritual palate.

Now *lectio* moves to the phase of *meditatio.* Traditionally, this has meant that you prayerfully repeat the word or phrase—

like the cow, you begin to ruminate. The meditative phase invites you to chew on the Scripture as real food, food for the journey—in this case, food for living with your illness. The gentle repetition may stir up associations from your memories and images from your experience, and even bring to mind other Scripture passages.

Your *meditatio* may be as simple and direct as a color presenting itself to your imagination, or it might be a cluster of thoughts, images, and feelings. The associations and stirrings that appear during *meditatio* will be unique to you, for this is the joining of your life and experience to the scriptural text. You may find it helpful to keep a journal and pen at hand to record the images, emotions, thoughts, memories, and associations that you discover.

Oratio

In the movement of *oratio*, you choose from among the images or memories or words that have come forth from *meditatio*. Then you create a prayer that speaks forth the feelings, thoughts, and intercessions associated with the meditative phase. One of my own spiritual directors has suggested that my intercession always move beyond my own situation to the more global or universal, reminding me that my own prayer is part of a lively whole. After you make and offer your prayer, once again enter the silence of *contemplatio*, thankfully resting in the divine Presence and allowing the word you've been given to become your flesh. This is a moment of being bathed in the regenerating silence of God's presence, the infinite silence from which all words are spoken. This last gentle movement reminds you that the context of your illness is always held within the infinite mercy and goodness of God—even when the raggedness of your own flesh makes that hard to know.

Contemplatio

This last movement brings you full circle to rest in the eternal silence of God. It's a moment of entrusting yourself, gratefully and peacefully, unto the arms of mercy. There is nothing to do, no work to perform. Simply allow yourself to be aware of what Thomas Merton, Trappist monk and writer, called "mercy within mercy within mercy."[8]

CONVERSATION AND *CONVERSATIO*

Applying *lectio divina* to Scripture allows you to come to the text not searching for answers but entering an ongoing conversation with God in Christ with trust and awareness. *Lectio* leads you out of narrow interpretation and individualistic focus, inviting you instead to know that "the beginning of wisdom is the most sincere desire for instruction" (Wis 6:17). Regular practice of *lectio* teaches you to listen for a word in all of life, and to beware of your own rigidities, certitudes, and quick solutions to pain and suffering. As you practice *lectio* with Scripture, you'll grow into a habit of regarding not only Scripture but life itself as a text to be encountered.

Because an ongoing conversation opens through *lectio*, things begin to change. You may notice changes in your perceptions and in your awareness. You may notice old behaviors and attitudes that you need to slough off. You may start to explore different ways of being and doing. In other words, through this holy conversation you enter what the Rule calls *conversatio morum*—ongoing transformation and conversion in Christ—and that's the real healing that your body and soul require. *Lectio divina* leads you into your baptismal identity as a living member of the Body of Christ. You discover that your life in faith is both more personal and more communal than you'd thought, that you're completely within the life of the Trinity, and that the life of the Trinity also indwells you. Your ongoing healing takes place as this wisdom takes hold and you're delivered from your soul's distress despite your body's ongoing dissipation.

This ongoing conversation happens because your soul's attitude is one of listening. It's an attitude that gives up control and simply receives—and in the receiving, you're changed. Think of your experience of daily conversation. When you're speaking and another person is truly listening, something beautiful and strange begins to occur. You hear your own voice saying what you know, feel, fear, desire. Another person hears this too, and in the hearing and receiving, each person is changed a bit. Something new happens, for in the receiving we are changed. Self-disclosure and honesty are possible, and trust begins to grow.

This sort of listening, in and of itself, may be deeply healing. It's the sort of listening that characterizes the conversation of *lectio divina*—the conversation that leads to conversion.

It's worth noting that this process isn't about curing your illness, restoring you to physical health. While that is always desired and hoped for, it's not always possible. In much of the recent literature about illness, there is a subtle (and sometimes overt) insistence that cure is the only mark of faith. Our baptismal life isn't oriented toward cure but toward the healing that comes with living within the gracious life of the living Trinity. Healing, which comes even when the body dies, is marked by deepening love for ourselves, for God, for our neighbors.

Healing of heart and soul bear the fruit of gentleness, hope, courage, joy, faith, truth. Cure in some cases may bypass healing; if the body is repaired and the heart and soul remain closed and stony, healing hasn't transpired. If the body is cured but the heart remains caught up in itself, healing hasn't happened. But if you can bear it, healing your heart's wounds through the mercy of God, through the experience of living with illness, may open the path of compassion in ways you never expected.

PRACTICE

Begin the practice of *lectio divina* with this exercise.

Materials needed: journal, writing materials

Some Preliminary Suggestions

1. Choose a place for your *lectio divina*. This could be your favorite rocker or a bench in the yard or your kitchen table. The important thing is to pick a place and regularly return to it. Over time, the place itself will help you enter the prayer. The chair will encourage you to get started; the room will become your sacred space. You may want to light a candle or burn some incense as a sacred act denoting that this time is set aside for a holy purpose.

2. Choose a time for your *lectio divina*. Are you more likely to be available—both inwardly and outwardly—in the morning? At noon? In the evening? At bedtime? Regular patterns of time help form the habit of *silencio*. Just as with regularity of place, regularity of time allows the prayerful disposition of the heart to grow. After weeks or months of practice, you may discover that as your prayer time approaches, the prayer calls to you and invites you to get started.

An Experience of *Lectio Divina*

SILENCIO

Start by noticing where your body is tense. I usually begin by breathing gently, then checking my neck and shoulders for tension. Give yourself time to relax, by breathing deeply and by flexing and relaxing any muscle group that feels tense.

Remembering that your silence is hopeful and open, enter it with the hope that a word intended for you will be spoken. The living God in whom you live and move and have your being awaits your attention. Enter with a willingness to be honest. If you are feeling tired and fretful, admit it. If one too many hospital visits or visitors has overwhelmed you, bring that awareness to *silencio*, too. Begin with the way you really are, not with the way you wish you were.

LECTIO

Read aloud slowly the portion of Psalm 139 that follows, pausing at the end of each verse. Breathe in and out, letting your breath and the words begin to interweave. Notice which word or phrase calls to you and captures "the ear of your heart."[9] Write it down in your journal.

LORD, you have searched me out and known me;
you know my sitting down and my rising up;
    you discern my thoughts from afar.
You trace my journeys and my resting-places
    and are acquainted with all my ways.
Indeed, there is not a word on my lips,
    but you, O LORD, know it altogether.
You press upon me behind and before
    and lay your hand upon me.

Such knowledge is too wonderful for me;
    it is so high that I cannot attain to it.
Where can I go then from your Spirit?
    Where can I flee from your presence?
If I climb up to heaven, you are there;
    If I make the grave my bed, you are there also.
If I take the wings of the morning
    and dwell in the uttermost parts of the sea,
Even there your hand will lead me
    and your right hand hold me fast.
If I say, "Surely the darkness will cover me,
    and the light around me turn to night,"
Darkness is not dark to you;
the night is as bright as the day;
    darkness and light to you are both alike.
For you yourself created my inmost parts;
    you knit me together in my mother's womb.
                    (*Book of Common Prayer*)[10]

MEDITATIO

Having noticed the word or phrase that calls your attention, gently repeat it aloud to yourself. As you pray this word or phrase, notice the following:
  • What feelings are you aware of?
  • What sort of response do you note in your body?
  • What memories or images come to you?
  • What other Scripture passages, prayers, hymns connect with this word or phrase?

These are simply suggestions. In any given time of *lectio divina* you probably won't experience all of them, nor should you

think that your experience is somehow impoverished if you
don't. You may also wish to offer some response that is not
listed here. Offer what is most genuine and suitable to your
physical and spiritual resources, given the presence of illness.

Note in your journal what comes to you in this time of meditating on the word or phrase.

ORATIO

Create a prayer from what has come to you during *meditatio*.
Elements of the prayer might include thanksgiving for what
you've discovered, petition for help or direction, intercession
for others and for the world. You may want to write the prayer
in your journal. The prayer may certainly take other forms (see
chapter 7).

CONTEMPLATIO

Finally, rest in the silence of God's presence in Christ. Let yourself become aware of the Christ in whom "all things hold
together" (Col 1:17).

You can follow this practice using a daily lectionary, such as
the one found in the *Book of Common Prayer*. As you repeat the
practice, it will become more and more familiar. The ordinary
daily rhythm of reading Scripture through the process of *lectio*
becomes your place for encountering the living Presence.

Remember that *lectio divina* invites you to ingest little
morsels of Scripture and to savor them, approaching the text as
a gourmet meal, not as a fast-food snack. Don't fret about not
reading enough, or not finishing whole books of Scripture in a
day. Just enter the conversation that unfolds between you and
the living God, who invites you to be glad to receive the Guest
who dwells within you, who chooses your broken body as a
place to abide.

CHAPTER 3

Our Lives and Our Bodies
as a Sacred Text

∼

READING OUR LIVES

"I can read her like a book."
"This chapter in his life is very hard."
Our language is filled with expressions that compare books and writing with our human experience. That's because the links are so strong. Intuitively we recognize that our lives are narratives. We speak of our life experience with the metaphors of pages, chapters, books: "I need to take a page from her life." "My life is an open book." "I can't read this situation."

Human beings are drawn to stories, and we tell them all the time, as we recount the daily minutiae of our lives to ourselves and one another. This process helps us sort through the barrage of details, make some sense of it, and proceed through the day. We also tell stories to illumine our lives, to deepen and broaden our awareness. We notice themes, nuances, and things that are asking for our attention.

Sometimes we may find ourselves telling and retelling a particular experience, often one that's particularly startling, disruptive, or grievous. But our attention may just as easily be captured by something very ordinary and heretofore unnoticed. As we attend to our own speech, we begin to hear ourselves recount the experience, trying to "read" the text, to find a narrative, to create some story line from the circumstance of our lives. Our storytelling—and retelling—reflects our intuitive ability and desire to read the text of our lives, interpreting as we go.

The telling and the reading of our lives are intimately intertwined. In the telling, we order the remembered events to make the text our own. Sometimes when we revisit a moment of great import from our lived experience, we discover that we "read" something new in that text. The text of our lives begins to acquire layers of meaning, rather than only one interpretation. Through the processes of prayer, conversation, journaling, spiritual direction, counseling, massage, yoga, dance, and therapy we revisit key moments, viewing them from the perspective of accrued life experience, and learning something different in the reading. We read, amplify, interpret, and reinterpret the text of the experience. It's an open-ended process, and it's remarkably similar to the practice of *lectio divina* with a written text.

So reading the text of an illness and even reading your body may not be as strange a notion as you might think. Probably, there have been moments in your life when you've already applied a process like *lectio* to your own life history. Once you become aware of your intuitive, human capacity to practice this sort of reading of life and illness, the process seems less alien.

For some, this will not be so much a new experience as an exercise in bringing intent and focus to a way of reflecting that you already do. Others will be trying this practice for the first time. But whatever your experience, think of the reading of the text of life and your illness as a form of human expression. This book invites you to notice your human response to life itself, to bring focused care to that response, and to offer that care with prayer and an open heart.

A BODY BROKEN

Reading the story of your life is a lot like reading the story of your illness. Your experience of a body that is weakened, stricken, or failing is the raw material of a story, a text waiting to be read with care and attention, then slowly interpreted. As a spiritual director I have spent hours listening to persons living with illness. I've been struck by the fact that the way they read their illness says a lot about how their lives are engaged, and brings to the surface implicit images of God that they need to examine or even discard. Regularly, I hear this kind of interpretation of an illness: "I must have done something bad or this wouldn't be happening," or "This must be punishment for my behavior." Though God is not explicitly mentioned in either of these readings, clearly they betray latent notions of God as the one who visits us with plague—a notion inconsistent with God as revealed in Jesus.

OUR LIVES AS SCRIPTURE

As anyone acquainted with Hebrew and Christian Scripture knows, story forms a large part of our sacred writings. The great, sweeping narratives of Scripture include themes of birth, death, plague, healing, deliverance, loneliness, community, and faithfulness, to name but a few. We're shaped by a tradition that impels us to hunt intuitively for stories. In Christian traditions that observe the seasons of Advent, Christmas, Epiphany, Lent, Easter, and Pentecost, every yearly cycle walks us through the sacred story of the coming of Jesus as a baby; his life in our midst; his crucifixion and resurrection; and his ongoing Incarnation through the church. Regular worship draws us into the scriptural story that shapes us, confounds us, challenges us, and calls us forth. The great narratives of the Hebrew Scriptures and the New Testament offer us ways of understanding what it is to be human, and how God reveals the divine presence in our lives and in our histories. We faintly remember that the telling of our tradition reminds us of who we are and gives us a sense of meaning.

Just so with our lives. One of the ways that we "read, mark, and learn" the experiences of our lives is by revisiting an experience, telling and retelling it, shaping the narrative as we speak, and allowing our perceptions to work their way into our words. The words, of course, are not the same as the experience. The words are already a translation of the reality we have lived.

This first translation of our reality into words takes time, reflection, and care—the sort of slow deliberation and absorption our culture tends to discourage. Instead, we're fed a diet of overstimulation and forced to gorge on our experience, and then rush to interpret it. The result is a confusion that's devastating, particularly for those who are ill. Simply coming to terms with the limitations of illness and with the enforced changes in schedule, nutrition, work, and play is disorienting. When the disorientation is compounded by a babble of facile readings of the text of the illness, real harm may result.

At the very least, the initial reading of the text of illness requires you to reacquaint yourself with a body that's changed.

In some cases, you may come to terms with the loss of an organ, or a breast, or even a limb. In other cases, your body's need for a certain pattern of nutrition, rest, and exercise may require a costly concentration on your new lifestyle. In addition, medication regimens that involve remembering times, dosages, and sequences will require an increasingly embodied practice for honoring your body's needs. These kinds of changes in behavior, identity, and lifestyle place you in the fluid and unsettling state of transition, where meaning is still emerging and your story is far from told. It's like discovering that the book underneath the dust jacket is a different text than the one you expected—but you have to read it anyway. You realize that the text, like your body and your life, is changed, maybe forever.

CREATIVE EXPRESSION AS PREPARATION FOR READING

After a very difficult surgery, Teresa found herself awaking from dreams that presented her with dark shapes. Within these deep blue-black shapes, she saw a point of light gleaming. She started with painting the shapes, time after time, and the light within the dark shape began to slowly grow wider. As she painted, she began to reflect on the emerging shape of her life following the surgery. At first, things had seemed dark and hopeless. Though she did not have a clear path at the time she was painting, the regular painting of the image began to give her a sense that there was hope in the midst of all of the inner turmoil following the surgery. Her reading of the text of the illness began with her openness to her dreams, and with her willingness to paint as a response.

For many of us, like Teresa, the first rendering of our experience may be in a nonverbal form, perhaps with paint or clay or movement, as a creative expression that allows deep feeling to come forth without words. The preliminary reading of the text of an illness may happen through image, color, form, music, or gesture. Because your body is the locus of the illness, it's uttering hints and intimations that invite a telling and a reading not limited to words.

Or perhaps your dreams will offer clues to the reading of your text. Try recording your dreams, then attending to the symbols within them, as a starting point.

LAYERS OF MEANING, COMMUNITIES OF STORY

When I began the long process of recovering from acute pancreatitis, I often found that I needed to hear myself tell the story to someone else to help me discover some hints of meaning. I also felt the need to write out the narrative for myself, and even to work with paint and clay, as a means of giving expression to an experience registered on a cellular level. Over time, some gifts emerged from what initially seemed to be nothing more than chaotic and painful disruption—gifts of awareness and gifts of questions. Revisiting of the events of my attack—the ride to the hospital in the ambulance, the hospitalization itself—offered bits and pieces of my own history that I could quilt together to help me find meaning in the experience of my illness.

The meaning of your illness may be embedded within your narrative, but it's not always easy to find. It may be hidden or covered over. Whatever meaning there may be in the experience of illness, it does not necessarily translate into the ready-made narrative structures of New Age fundamentalism or Christian literalism. In fact, those applications can be thoroughly destructive. To decide too quickly about the import of an illness can

obstruct the faithful and patient listening for wisdom and discernment. Something flat and dried up is substituted for the
slow disclosure of what is needed for true healing.

Consider the story of my friend Ed. Diagnosed with
melanoma, a potentially lethal form of skin cancer, he found
himself haunted at first by the surgical wound created when the
malignant mole was excised. He had had other surgeries, and
the wounds had not haunted him, but this cut—even though it
didn't hurt, even though it wasn't ugly—nagged at his awareness. It became a symbol for him—but of what? As he awaited
the results of the pathology tests, he began to tell his spiritual
director about this unease with the wound, discovering that he
thought of the melanoma as a "black hole." In telling the story
of the diagnosis, the initial test, and the excision, he began to
realize even before his surgery, he was aware that depression
was approaching. What, Ed wondered, did the symbolism of
the darkness, the blackness—the black hole—portend?

That's when Ed and his spiritual director began to reflect on
the text of the illness. His reflection was also a reading of the
text of his body. Provoked by the incision itself, by the stitches
and the skin swelling around them, he was "reading" his body,
and the reality of the loss of a piece of his own flesh shocked
him every time he looked in the mirror. The embodied fact of
his own vulnerability would not leave him alone. Ed began to
talk about his fear of living the life he felt he was called to live,
and of hard decisions he would need to make. He would need
to leave his present job and confront some serious personal
issues. He thought of the mandorla of flesh that the doctor
removed, and he began to wonder if there were behaviors he
needed to cut out. As he read the text of his wounded flesh, he
began to ask foundational questions about his values, his
death, his life.

If you live with illness, you know something about Ed's experience: the "other" in the form of illness takes up residence in your body, radically changing the story of your life, and you feel compelled to talk about it. Again and again in support groups and prayer groups, I hear persons living with illness speak of their intrinsic desire to tell the narrative of their experience, and for their narrative to be heard by listeners with a heartfelt understanding of the issues concerning identity, work, meaning, family, health. Illness changes everything, and often the disruption leads to changes in employment, relationship, self-awareness. Telling your narrative allows you to know yourself anew, as you weave a fabric of community with those who listen to your story. We need one another to help us listen for the deeper meaning, for hope, in the midst of the dislocation and disorientation that illness may bring.

"YOU KNIT ME TOGETHER"

Throughout our history, Christians have had a thoroughly ambivalent relationship with our bodies. From the early centuries of the church, we departed from our Judaic heritage, which tended to honor the body as part of the divine creation. Adopting an attitude that often seems misogynist at worst and wrongheaded at best, the Church began to insist on the subjugation of the flesh, and immoderate measures were often taken in the hopes that being harsh with the body would free the soul. While the historical situation is complex and the context in which these attitudes arose encouraged this perspective, the point of this book is to bring to awareness the sacred nature of the body as a part of the God's ongoing creative activity.

Our Judaic heritage gives us a clear mandate: we're to receive our bodies as works that have been intimately fashioned by

God. Psalm 139 reminds us that the living God knit us together in our mothers' wombs, implying that our very flesh is the handiwork of God. The New Testament, too, affirms the sacredness of our bodies. The central proclamation of the New Testament, that Jesus is the Word made flesh, proclaims that divinity embraces our embodied nature, even to the point of putting on the weakest and most distorted aspects of humanity. God cares for everybody—literally, every human body. Though they might be involved in sinful behavior, they're still expressions of God's own creative and redemptive love. We are embodied souls because we are so created, the loving works of this God who fashions us with great care. We need to reclaim this gospel proclamation, particularly when illness is involved.

The body that God created is a little world, a microcosm. Within it, fluids course, transporting nutrients, oxygen, blood. Our circulatory, nervous, and lymphatic systems; our liver, heart, intestines, brain, kidney, lungs—all of our organs—continually perform little miracles of transformation, converting food to energy, oxygen to carbon dioxide.

Many of us have been schooled to think of the body as a machine, rather than as an organic whole, continually uttered into being by God. Our Judaic heritage teaches us that all that is created is spoken forth by God. It's a fine scriptural metaphor that also tells us something of the creative divine work that never ceases—for if it did, everything would cease to exist. The living God speaks each particle of matter into being—each cell, each body, each person. When we become ill, we may feel deeply betrayed by the disobedient bodies we dwell in. When I was first hospitalized, several people asked me, "How could someone so healthy become so ill so quickly?" It's an easy, reasonable question, and one that needs to be asked, for diagnostic purposes if nothing else.

But there's another, deeper question: What wondrous creation is this body that can withstand so much pain and disorder
and still continue to function? What is at work in this flesh that
I take for granted that allows me to continue living? How is it
possible that I have taken this microcosm that is my body so
for granted?

Illness is without a doubt disconcerting, disturbing, perhaps
cause for despair. Illness can also serve as a means to awareness.
Reflecting on the ability of the body to heal, to keep going in
the face of chronic ailments, to repair after chemotherapy and
radiation, may lead us to become aware that this body truly is
called to be a temple of the Holy Spirit, as Saint Paul put it. Our
perception may shift. The body is neither the betrayer nor the
machine but a sacramental sign of the creating, redeeming,
sanctifying work of God. We become aware that our bodies are
not in our complete control; at the same time we have a call to
be good stewards of these bodies, to care for them as good gifts
from a good God—even when the bodies are afflicted and
pain-stricken.

PRACTICE

Encountering Your Body

Materials needed: a journal and a pen or some colored markers

SILENCIO

Having chosen your particular place and time for your practice,
sit comfortably in a chair or lie at full length on the floor on a
padded surface (such as a folded blanket or quilt). If either of
these positions will not work for your body, choose a position
that allows you to be relaxed but attentive.

Begin by breathing slowly. Gently focus your attention on your breath without trying to control the rate of breathing. Note the way the air feels as it enters your nostrils, flows down your throat and into your lungs. If your breathing is shallow, carefully breathe a little more deeply with each breath. Give yourself time to become accustomed to this rhythm. Then let yourself become aware of the wave of oxygen as it enters, coursing through your limbs down to your toes, out to your fingers. Notice the ebb of the wave with the exhalation of the carbon dioxide.

LECTIO

Having become aware of your breath, now let your awareness go to these various organs of your body:

brain
lungs
heart
stomach
pancreas
liver
intestine
kidneys
bladder
genitals

As you breathe, give thanks to God for each of these organs, and for any other part of your body that you choose (perhaps your bones or nervous system or lymphatic system). With the breathing, focus your awareness on each organ listed, allowing yourself to be mindful of its ongoing work within the larger whole. Take as much time as you need to attend to each organ. Notice if there is a particular area of the body that calls your attention, or that has a particular significance, or that brings memories forth.

MEDITATIO

Choose one organ from those you have attended. Kindly focus your awareness on that particular part of your body, adding this prayer: "I will thank you because I am marvelously made" (Ps 139:13). For example, perhaps your attention has rested upon your kidney. Breathing slowly, let your awareness focus on your kidneys, while repeating silently or aloud, "I will thank you because I am marvelously made." There is no clever formula for matching the words to the breath; just let that happen as naturally as you can.

As your attention remains with one particular organ, notice if you have any feelings, fears, misgivings, anxieties, questions, or thanksgivings. What memories come to you? Concerns? Associations? Allow yourself time to pay attention to images or colors. Perhaps a line from a hymn, or a song, or a poem will come to you during this time of focusing.

ORATIO

While remaining in a comfortable position, gather your thoughts and feelings into a prayer. Give thanks for your body, for one particular organ and its ceaseless working. Become mindful of those in the healing professions who help persons who have an illness that affects this particular organ. Pray for those those who are ill and those who care for them.

Finally, allow yourself to become aware of the deep connections of the human family, for we are very much alike in the structure and arrangement of our physical selves. Let this connection enter your awareness; pray for the whole human family.

CONTEMPLATIO

After your prayer, let yourself receive the silence once again. Imagine your body encompassed by a gentle, illumining light. Rest in this illumined silence as long as you wish.

Some Practical Suggestions

1. Once your prayer practice has come to a close, you may want to make some notes in your journal about what unfolded for you during this process. Perhaps you will want to make sketches or paintings, or fashion a work from clay, of the particular organ that drew your attention. Perhaps your creative medium is writing, or dance, or music. These creative responses are an extended form of your prayer.

2. You may want to return to this meditation from time to time, focusing on a different organ. Or you may want to return to the same organ, offering prayer and attention to a particular area of the body that is hurt or weakened. Adapt the meditation to suit your needs, your gifts of creative expression and your own capacities for attention.

Note: If you are in a very debilitated condition, you may want to do this meditation in shortened form. Rather than reviewing the whole body and its various organs in the *oratio* phase, you may want to focus on a specific organ from the outset.

Your Words in Flesh

You will need a friend to help with this practice.

Materials needed: a 6–7-foot length of butcher paper and colored markers or paint or pastels

1. Start by lying on the butcher paper on your back. Invite a friend to draw an outline of your body on the butcher paper. If you cannot lie on your back, adapt the exercise by outlining a foot or a hand—whatever might be possible, given your physical condition.

2. Once the outline is completed, place it where you can color the paper. Using colored markers or paint or pastels, begin coloring the space within and without. Don't worry about staying within the lines; you may in fact find that you want to color over the lines. You do not have to do this all at one sitting. You may want to spend some time on the coloring.

3. As you add color to this impression of your body on paper, pay attention to what emerges in the design. Notice if you discover places that seem to have no color. When you reach a stopping point, place the paper on the wall or in some other area where you may gaze at it.

4. Write down any impressions, questions, or insights that come to you from this exercise.

5. Form a prayer from this experience. Bring into the prayer some of what you have discovered in this practice. End with a thanksgiving. For example: "O God, I did not realize that my body was so full of color. Thank you for teaching me." Or: "Word made Flesh, speak to me in this flesh, speak to me in the color, speak to me in the experience." Your prayer doesn't need to be elaborate. Simple and direct expression is fine.

6. From time to time, return to this exercise, either by starting with a new outline of your body or by embellishing the picture you have already created.

CHAPTER 4

Silencio

~

SILENCE AND ILLNESS

A s we discovered in the overview of *lectio divina* in Chapter 2, the first step in the process is silence. But in the context of acute or chronic illness, silence may be hard to come by, at least the kind of silence that is primarily external. Illness, by its very nature, disrupts our accustomed patterns and routines and casts us into noisy, crowded, busy places—hospitals, doctors' offices, exam rooms, and treatment rooms. Then there's the "noise of the soul" that can occur during illness, as things inside, both physically and spiritually, are stirred up. The major changes that illness brings disturb and destroy our identities, practices of prayer, and ways of living.

Even those with years of practice in centering prayer or yoga or
another prayer discipline may find themselves feeling overwhelmed in the context of illness.

Recollection

The silence that underlies, surrounds, and upholds the practice
of *lectio divina* is marked by what our tradition calls "recollection." To recollect is to re-collect, to gather the bits and pieces of
experience, thoughts, and emotions. It's a moment of ingather-
ing, a pause to reclaim the parts of myself that have been dis-
tracted or distressed during the course of the day or the latest
blood test or doctor's exam. In a way, this pause for recollection
lets us catch up with the experiences of the day—or it lets the
experience of the day catch up with us. This is necessary if we
are to pray through the text of our bodies in such a way that
we are listening for God's presence through the events—even
the traumas—of the day.

The Silence of Sabbath

In addition, this silence is not something we create in and of
ourselves. This silence is that which is grounded in Sabbath rest,
in the commending of ourselves unto the infinite re-creative
presence of God. Again our Hebraic roots give us some cues.
The Orthodox Jewish practice of regularly observing *shabbat*
serves as a reminder that we come from God and we return to
God. We allow ourselves to be held within the arms of mercy, to
rest in God's eternal presence. Consequently, we are not *working* to create silence. We are stopping, recollecting, paying attention to the infinite silence of God from which the word that is
our created life is uttered.

In the Gospel of John, Jesus invites us to abide in him (John 15:4–7). This abiding is a kind of Sabbath awareness, an embodied knowing that the living Presence surrounds, indwells, re-creates, and infuses us. When we abide in Christ, we may allow ourselves to be held by the One who has made us, who loves us, who redeems us. In abiding, we find that no words are absolutely necessary. In fact, words may get in the way. We allow ourselves to stop, to steep in a silence brimming with God's presence.

Particularly when you're ill, this moment of allowing the perception of the eternal, merciful, and creative silence of God to greet you may be a source of great healing. Our culture habituates us to noise, to rushing, to an inhuman pace. When illness forces you to stop—to spend days or months or even years in diminished activity—there may be a hidden mercy. As you grieve the life you've lost, you may also discover seeds of the life you've been given, a strange, different life that feels as if it's not truly yours. But in time, you realize that your new life has its own integrity and its own purpose, despite being framed by physical impairment. Your life accompanied by illness may bring you to a steadier awareness of the silence of *shabbat*, this silence of God's eternal presence, in which you are renewed and replenished, even when your flesh is failing. The life marked by illness may bring you the peculiar gift of abiding, for as you honor the needs of your broken body, you must stop and receive, be vulnerable and dependent.

Stillness and Pain

A quality of interior stillness allows recollection and the silence to happen. But interior stillness is no easy feat. Even when you're externally still and silent, it may be hard to still the

clamor of your body in pain, or ease the panic of a dreaded—
and often-repeated—procedure. Those are times when the possibility of inner silence and stillness seem like a fantasy. When
you're sick, there may indeed be moments, or days, or months
when such stillness and silence are beyond your capacity. Be
honest about this. Don't impose heroic spiritual goals when you
need every bit of vitality to mend your bruised flesh. If you're in
intractable pain, any focused practice may be physically and
spiritually impossible.

But even in the middle of real physical distress, some people
report a gift of silence and stillness, a sense of being acutely
present to a particular trauma or course of events. This is not
stillness in the sense of the cessation of exterior movement;
rather it is stillness in the sense of encountering an infinite
Presence beyond words.

ONE WOMAN'S PRACTICE OF SILENCE

So, how are those of us who live with illness to imagine silence
in the midst of our particular, peculiar circumstances? Linda,
an older woman who had endured some weeks in an intensive-
care unit, found that her life as a musician helped her reflect on
silence in the midst of all the beeping machinery that was intimately connected to her body. When she encountered a
moment of awareness, she realized there were rhythms in the
beepings that were oddly like patterns in music. Because of her
training, she started listening to the noises in a different way—
sometimes, she even heard the silence between the beeps. As she
began healing and neared the end of her stay in the ICU, she
had a sense of the deep silence of God. Though her body still
hurt and her attention was shortened by pain-killing drugs,
Linda noticed a silence that was not just the absence of noise,

nor even the pause between beeps. Through the veil of her body's stresses, she perceived—not with physical sight but with intuition—a Presence. It wasn't an angelic apparition or a sense of a particular being, but a brief, acute awareness that God permeated everything in her room, yet was in no way reduced to that room. Theologically speaking, she became aware of God's immanence, of the nearness and immediacy of the divine.

ALLOWING THE SILENCE TO FIND US

When an acute illness kidnaps you, the initial moments, hours, or days may be a blur. It may be very difficult, if not impossible, to concentrate long enough to listen to anything except the direct instructions of medical personnel. And the sheer shock of an acute event may leave you unable to listen. Yet somehow, many persons do manage to listen. They discover upon reflection that there has been a gift given, but perhaps not received. These persons have encountered a spiritual sense.

We have five physical senses: sight, touch, hearing, taste, smell. But we also have spiritual senses—spiritual sight, touch, hearing, taste, smell—that operate beyond our conscious awareness. The tradition of the early Church, for instance, recognized hearing as a way to listen for the deeper truth, presence, and connection that occurred outside of human control. And often those spiritual senses are hard at work even during the terrible onset of illness. In listening to the stories of people who have lived through this experience, I have found that with careful recollection, they've often discovered that they knew more than they realized. Chances are, this awareness came later, after the shock wore off and the pain diminished. Yet some people register this sensory awareness in the moment, perhaps because the intensity of the pain focuses their attention. In either case,

the practice of *silencio* is less a matter of a person directly willing the silence to happen than it is a matter of the silence greeting the person, either in the moment or at a later time of
remembering. This type of spiritual listening requires waiting
for the remembered silence to make itself known. It can't be
forced and it cannot be rushed. It comes as gift.

Chronic or Long-Term Illness

When you're living with illness—when this strange and unin-
vited "other" is no longer a guest but a permanent resident in
the housing of your body—silence may come unbidden and
unwelcome. That's how it was for me in the first months of my
recovery from pancreatitis. Physically, I was in a weakened state
that destroyed my sense of identity and caused my aching body
to be easily stressed by activities I'd never thought about, like
digestion. Learning to eat very small amounts of food every two
or three hours was especially hard not only because of my
diminished appetite but also because of my fear of more pain. I
was at home by myself during most of the day, and silence—a
long, empty, threatening silence—was the norm.

Then a physician friend of mine began to regularly bring me
tapes of a variety of classical music from his extensive classical
CD collection. The music, I discovered, served to help me find
the silence. While this may seem odd, the fact was that the classical music helped me to relax, and therefore to concentrate.
The music pointed beyond itself; the melodic sounds somehow
soothed the fear that tended to stalk me, especially at night.

The music became the way I could prepare for a real, hopeful silence. I found that when a piece of music came to an end,
I could befriend the welling silence that ensued. The music
offered me a rhythm that was not panicked, and entering that

rhythm was a kind of anointing. No words were necessary. The music spoke volumes, easing my fear and lifting my depression. I began to know—and desire—the silence of God from which the music poured forth.

Music is just one way of entering silence. One man I know, recovering from extensive surgery followed by radiation and chemotherapy, found that when he sat on his front porch, rather than inside his house, silence came as a blessing and a preparation for prayer. Being outside helped him enter the silence. He discovered over time that some of his hospital experiences had made him claustrophobic, and that for him, silence and freedom were intimately linked. As a consequence, his very body seemed to need the fresh air and open space of his porch, rather than the enclosure of his bedroom. Sitting in a rocking chair, with pillows to support his body, he could trust the open space enough to let go of some of the fear and tension. His body seemed to ease in the open space, but others may find they need enclosure.

The issue of space can be exceedingly important in entering silence when you're ill. Find the space that's right for you. Take physical limitation into account, but be alert to the spaces that invite you to enter Sabbath rest and enter the deep, replenishing silence of God.

Finding Silence in the Exams

Even in the midst of regularly undergoing diagnostic testing, from blood work to CAT scans, you still have opportunities to observe silence. Take my friend Elizabeth, for example. She's trained herself to use regular motions and sensations—the swabbing of her elbow, the tying of the tourniquet, the lab tech's feeling for a vein—as cues to move into silence. Because she's relaxing rather than tensing, Elizabeth's practice no doubt does help with the actual drawing of blood, but this practice also allows her to enter into the moment from a prayerful perspective. Sometimes her prayers are funny: "Dear God, you are needling me yet again." Sometimes they're observant: "Bless the company that makes the needles so that the blood can be drawn." And sometimes they're fearful: "Please let the white count be better." She has also developed the courage to ask the lab technician to pause for a moment before actually inserting the needle. For Elizabeth, this makes the regular drawing of blood feel less like an exercise in which, to use her words, "I just feel like a hunk of meat."

Elizabeth comes to the test with a disposition of the heart that looks for a moment of silence, even in the stress of the blood test. That orientation allows her to go through the regular testing with a sense that she is being accompanied by God even in this piercing of her veins. It does not mean she has no pain, or that the needle always hits the vein on the first try. It does mean that she has entered the moment of having her blood drawn with a different orientation to the experience.

The Exam Room

If you've lived with illness, you know the routine of the exam room. You're called from the waiting area to be weighed and measured, then taken to a private exam room. Then you wait for the physician to appear, chart in hand, to begin the latest phase of the ongoing conversation. Once again, the environment in which you wait is not completely silent. Nurses and physicians passing in the hall exchange greetings, information, concerns. Phones ring. Sometimes lab results are called out from a nurse's station to a waiting doctor.

Sometimes, you can hear conversations in an adjacent exam room, and you might find yourself, unwittingly, listening to the tone of voice, the questions and answers happening next door. How can you encounter silence without eavesdropping on a fellow patient's private conversation? One woman I know uses a technique she learned from her Lamaze method births of over twenty years ago. She finds a focal point in the exam room and concentrates on it. It might be a knob on a cabinet, or a pencil on a countertop—for her, a neutral object works best, though for others a more complicated object, like an anatomical chart, might be a better choice. Once she has selected the focal point, she begins noticing her breath. Most of the time, she realizes that it's shallow, for the experience of submitting to the exam, despite the kindness of this particular physician, elicits too much adrenaline. Once she's aware of this, though, she begins to breathe more slowly, letting the breath move deeply into her trunk and limbs with each inhalation. As the breathing begins to call her attention, she finds that the silence, full of Presence, begins to make itself known. The chatter has not stopped in the hallway. The exam in the next room continues. But the breathing that is a form of communion, recalling Jesus' saying "You [are] in me and I in you," (John 14:20) allows her to remember the context of divine life that permeates and sustains all. The room in which she sits, furnished with blood pressure cuff, charts, and probes, becomes a little prayer closet. The stark reality of physical distress is still present, yet present within the encompassing reality of God.

One man who regularly uses prayer beads during his morning prayer has discovered that taking them with him to the regular exams demanded by his cancer has helped him return to the inner silence. In his case, the touch of the beads grounds him.

He's handled them for years, so his fingers know their texture and weight intimately. As he waits for his oncologist, in that threshold moment of wondering what the next hour will bring, he has found that just holding the beads allows him to recover the silence that he practices every morning. The familiar silence of his regular prayer follows him, through the agency of the beads, into spaces fraught with the unknown.

Sometimes, though, you just can't bring anything along to your test—no prayer beads, no medal, no adornment of any kind. Marie solved this problem when she went to the hospital for a CAT scan checking for the return of a tumor. While she was undergoing the test, the friend who had driven her to the hospital wore the woman's small gold cross on a chain around her neck. As she was being tested, Marie prayerfully imagined her friend waiting in solidarity, wearing the cross. The gurney of the CAT scan became a symbol of being supported and upheld, a means of being grounded in the silence from which all creation is uttered into being. Though the experience of being scanned was also a continual conversation with the technician, in the silent moments between words, the grounding of the friend's presence and prayer connected to the silence from which the living Word is spoken.

PRACTICE

"For God Alone My Soul in Silence Waits"

1. Find a comfortable position. For some, this may mean lying in a reclining position. For others, it might mean getting comfortable in a wheelchair. Find a position and a place that work best for you.

Bring your attention to your breath. Inhale with gentleness, slowly letting your lungs expand. Pause for a count of two, then exhale gently. Breathe this way for several minutes, letting yourself become aware of the expansion of your chest. As you breathe, direct your attention to any places in your body that are aching or holding tension. Breathe into those places by focusing your attention on them while steadily inhaling and exhaling.

Note: If you live with a chronic pulmonary problem of any sort, adjust the breathing exercises in this book to your particular ability and level of comfort.

2. Having let the breathing rhythm establish itself, begin praying silently: "For God alone my soul waits in silence" (Ps 62:1). Stay with the prayer for as long as you wish. Let your body relax into the prayer and be upheld by it.

3. After praying the line from the psalm for a while, continue to breathe, but let the prayer move into silence. Picture yourself upheld and supported in whatever way is meaningful for you—by friends, by a strong hammock, by a sturdy tree (various images that have been given to some of the people under my spiritual direction). Notice the Presence that fills the silence.

4. Return to this simple practice regularly. It is completely portable, and will go with you to whatever exam room, diagnostic procedure, or hospital you need to enter.

Checking Your Pulse

No matter what brings you to the doctor, chances are somebody will take your pulse. It's a way to check not only the rhythmic throbbing of your arteries, but also the silence between the beats, that small and necessary pause between the contraction of the chambers of your heart.

1. Following the instructions above, situate yourself comfortably and begin noticing your breathing. Allow the breath to steady and deepen.

2. Place the index and middle finger of your right hand on the left side of your neck, over your artery (or use your left hand on the right side of your neck—whatever is easiest). Through the touch of the fingers notice the beat of your pulse. Don't count beats—just notice the pulse. Pay attention for several minutes, noticing the slight pause between beats. Addressing that momentary silence, begin to pray, "In You I live and move and have my being."

Pray this way without hurry or tension for a time. When you're ready, gently remove your fingers from your neck and remain still, continuing to pray, "In You I live and move and have my being." Then return to silence and deep breathing. Notice any changes in your body, in your awareness, in your muscles.

3. Use your journal to note your impressions from the time of your prayer. Return to this exercise as needed; you can use it in a variety of places. Keep a record of your perceptions of your body, of the presence of God, of the silence.

Varieties of Silence

Make note of the varieties of silences and spaces your illness has acquainted you with. Start a page in your journal for each type of silence, each kind of space—for example, the chatty silence of the exam room with thin walls, the silence of being put on hold while waiting to speak with the doctor on the phone, the silence of some diagnostic tests. In these contexts, begin practicing one or two ways of praying listed in the previous section.

As you continue to practice in these spaces make notes in your journal about your own variations on these suggested ways of leaning into the silence of God.

The Silence between the Notes

You will need a CD player or a cassette player for this exercise, with music of your choosing. Some composers whose music has helped me and others move to silence are J. S. Bach, Giovanni Palestrina, Arvo Pärt, John Tavener, Henryk Górecki, John Rutter. I also recommend Gregorian chant and Taizé chant. With the exception of chant, I would suggest using music that is without words, as it leads more gently to the silence.

1. Listen to your music, breathe so that you inhabit the rhythms of the music. With chant this is fairly easy to discern. With other works, find the pattern of breathing that fits with the melody.

2. Imagine that the music is upholding you, as if you were resting on a vital, resilient river of sound. Let yourself be in the music fully. Notice where the music registers in your body. Do you feel it in your head? Your heart? Your lungs? Your gut? Your genitals? Does the music evoke color or shape?

3. As the music comes to an end, let yourself receive the ensuing silence. Rest in the great silence from which all music comes, including the inner music of your own body.

4. Repeat this practice as often as you wish, perhaps returning to the same music again and again, perhaps listening to different composers. Notice your body's response. After the music ends, allow the silence to envelop you.

CHAPTER 5

Lectio

~

WHAT IS THIS TEXT?

I n the early years of the church, when texts were laboriously copied by hand and many people were illiterate, this phase of *lectio divina* was a process of recalling the Scripture rather than reading it. Hearing was more important then, and so was learning from memory. As the Scripture took up residence within the person, becoming one with the person through regular repetition, the phrase or line would come forth in prayer. The person praying began to have within himself or herself an inner text, ready for the direction of the Holy Spirit. The remembered Scripture could come unbidden, a gracious bit of direction during a time of discernment. Or the Scripture might be more consciously invited through linking it to a particular activity or time of day, as we do with the Episcopal practice of praying the Daily Office. The opening lines of Morning Prayer, taken from Psalm 51:15, "Lord, open our lips/And our mouth shall proclaim your praise,"[11] have become part of our remembered scriptural heritage, as well as the heritage of the early years of the devotional practice of the Church. Our illness offers us another scripture to read and internalize, another scripture through which the Spirit speaks.

Literal Interpretations of Illness

Just as in the early church *lectio* was accomplished through recalling and remembering Scripture, so too with the experience of falling ill and living with illness. We are invited to recall and remember. The text in this case is the text of the body, particularly this afflicted body. The body—wedded to the soul and shaping us as unique persons—is itself a living word, spoken into being by the God in whom we live and move and have our being. This living text of the various microcosms of our organs and bodily systems is also a living metaphor, a figure of divine speech that invites our listening. Yet that meaning cannot and should not be assumed, prescribed, or dictated.

Like any rich and intricately detailed text, the body cannot and should not be reduced to one layer of meaning. Have you ever had a high school English teacher who proclaimed the one—and only—meaning of a poem or story? Alternative meanings were not acceptable. Have you ever experienced the literalism of some within the Christian community as they interpret Scripture? Both cases are examples of reductionist thinking, where meaning has been reduced to a sound bite, hindering us from knowing the deeper, fuller meaning. When we read on only the simplest, most literal of levels, we often miss the point.

Sadly, this sort of interpretation has also invaded the realm of health and spirituality. Guides to interpreting illness are everywhere, leading those who are ill and vulnerable to simplistic and sometimes guilt-ridden ways of reading their experience. Some authors, for example, imply that emphysema results not so much from environmental toxins or cigarette smoking, but from not breathing one's life. Breast cancer signals trouble with womanhood, and so on. While there may be clues about the text of an illness in the organ affected, it is harmful to reduce the experience to this level of direct cause and effect.

From within Christian quarters, a different kind of fundamentalism can reign. This is the kind of belief and practice that subjects the sick person to continuous, smug evaluation. Comments such as "You know, if you just prayed harder, your bipolar disorder would be healed" or "God has given you the cancer so that you can learn a lesson" have behind them a theology that has little to do with the Trinity of Love. These comments are based, rather, on fear and uneasiness with mortality. It is fear and anxiety that tend to force us into simplistic interpretations, whether we are interpreting Scripture, our lives, or our illnesses.

Again and again, I hear from those under my spiritual direction and from those who participate in my classes that these sorts of comments abound. Because a person who lives with physical or mental affliction is already experiencing a degree of distancing, these comments can be especially injurious. However, when two or three persons whose lives are marked by illness come together, they can support one another in Christ by peeling away interpretations that are false and misleading, if not downright punitive. They can hear what one another's bodies

and illnesses are saying. They can offer one another a little community in which to practice *lectio* of the illness.

Discovering the Text

The body, which is a living word from the Word, is a text with
many layers of meaning. These layers await our taking the time
to encounter them, to listen to them, and to let them illumine
one another. This discovery of the text of the body allows us to
befriend the body, to perceive this flesh as a wonder, even when
we are engaging in terribly difficult medical regimens. Illness,
from this perspective, is part of a lifelong encounter with the
divine mystery. The person who chooses to engage this reading
of the text of illness will not so much be looking to a symbol
dictionary or the latest version of "Your illness means . . ." from
the best-seller list. The person who chooses this path of *lectio*
will be entering a process of deeply listening to the experience,
to the body, to the life that unfolds through physical diminishment. This can be daunting. It's like taking off from a well-
known shore and setting sail for a new land. It's a little like
going on a pilgrimage.

THE METAPHOR OF PILGRIMAGE: GETTING INTO THE CORACLE

From the early church in the Celtic lands (now Scotland, Wales,
Ireland, Brittany, Cornwall, and the Isle of Man) we receive a
version of pilgrimage that serves well as a metaphor for this *lectio* of the body. In Celtic tradition, rather than starting off with
a destination in mind, such as Jerusalem or Rome, pilgrims got
in a little boat known as a coracle, round in shape with no oars.
Once on board, the pilgrim trusted the currents of the sea or

the river to take the little boat to a destination hid with Christ. The current was the means by which the pilgrim was brought to the "place of resurrection," the geographical spot where the pilgrim would live out his remaining days and eventually die. But the "place of resurrection" is the place where we encounter the living Christ who has burst the tomb and whose radiant presence frees us from all imprisoning and demeaning interpretations of our lives.

I point to the Celtic pilgrims because the engagement with the text of illness may lead away from well-known shores and familiar interpretations, too. This engagement, without claiming to offer answers or solutions or definitive spiritual insight, calls us to muster the same sort of courage that a Celtic pilgrim needed to have. Setting off toward Jerusalem or Rome was a pilgrimage fraught with danger, but at least the destination was a given. Getting into the coracle involved a degree of trust that most of our religious training has succeeded in extinguishing. When I offer this metaphor for the life of faith in classes, inevitably there is a sharp intake of breath and a chorus of "OH!" We are startled that living faithfully might look like this kind of trust. We have tended to think of faith as a set of propositions about doctrinal truth that we need to affirm intellectually. The metaphor of the pilgrimage in the coracle reminds us that faith and trust are two faces of the same reality, and that faith involves our selves, our souls, and our bodies.

This sort of trust is precisely what we need to honestly engage the experience of illness and to forsake the ready answers that our health-conscious culture provides. This sort of trust invites us out of tombs of literalistic attitudes toward living with illness, into the freedom of the place of our resurrection. We are invited, through this sort of reflection, to befriend the fact of our mortality and creatureliness. We are led to remember, as the Benedictine Rule counsels, to keep death at our shoulder daily. This is not a morbid practice. It is simply an honest one.

For many persons who have been living not only with the stress of illness but also with the stress of others' anxiety for a cure, this trusting may come slowly. But it may also feel dizzily freeing. In my classes, even among those living with a so-called terminal diagnosis, some experience a real quickening of spirit, when their own deep intuitions are called forth. When the truth begins to be spoken in love, they may experience "bright sadness," a term used by the early Church to encompass joy and pain simultaneously, without negating either. It's ultimately an embrace of the Christian proclamation that even at the grave we make our song: "Alleluia, alleluia, alleluia!" Getting into the coracle, entrusting ourselves to the currents of divine love, and seeking the place of our resurrection implies that we are embracing the truth of our mortality—we wouldn't need a place of resurrection if we weren't mortal. As we learn to number our days, and to remember that each person's days are numbered, living, even living with an illness, becomes a process of moving toward the infinite love from which we were birthed.

THE CULTURE OF BEING HEALTHY

In the United States today we live in a culture frightened to the core by illness. Health is upheld as a value, and for good reason. We benefit when we honor our bodies through a good balance of work, rest, exercise, and play. We are healthier when we pay attention to nutrition, tending to the ways that we feed ourselves and our children. Preventive medicine has always been a wise course, and we are remembering its virtues.

At the same time, underneath our obsession with health is a lurking fear of death. As a culture, we tend to deny the fact that we will die, that our days are numbered. We persist in behaviors that keep us from honoring the aging process—from a perpetual depiction of lithe, too slender, almost naked young female bodies in advertising to a strange fixation on the whiteness of our teeth. I am convinced that in part our tendencies to apply various literalisms to illness come from this distress about mortality. The underlying fear and anxiety about dying are not directly engaged, so they roil around inside us, and push us toward simplistic and impulsive solutions. But solutions are for problems; life is for living, even when the living is marked by the limitation of physical or mental impairment.

Even the church participates in the strange amnesia of forgetting that we are creatures. Our church programming endlessly cranks out events and classes geared toward ceaseless activity. We behave as if being still, reflecting, and keeping silence were not an essential part of Christian spiritual practice. We tend to encourage busyness rather than reflection, activity rather than rest in God's providence. As church newsletters tout events, congregants assume that living the life of faith means going to meetings and shoehorning more activity into an already overscheduled day.

This incessant doing tends to produce simplistic interpretations and shallow answers. It also subtly implies that if your life isn't characterized by productivity and action, you're not very valuable. However, as Roman Catholic priest and author Henri Nouwen has pointed out, the New Testament is not concerned with productivity. The New Testament is concerned with fruitfulness, an organic and mysterious bearing of life that comes from the root of our being.

Recalling and Remembering

Within this larger context, the practice of *lectio divina* with the body, with a physical or mental malady, invites you to recall and remember. You can't rush, and you can't expect a quick-fix remedy for the dilemmas of living with illness. *Lectio divina* applied to the body invites the quiet, deep listening that leads us into the freedom of the God who brought us into being, who knit us together in our mothers' wombs. In a way, when a person begins to practice this kind of recalling, this initial reading of the text of the illness, it is not unlike being led out of captivity into freedom. In this case, the captivity is that of solutions, answers, and meanings too quickly applied to the experience of living with illness, a captivity that squelches the imagination and binds it with rules. Faithful practice of *lectio* with illness, on the other hand, allows the Holy Spirit within us to participate in the search for meaning.

This practice of recalling also may take us into memories we would just as soon not revisit. Often the experience of falling ill is deeply distressing, and the recalled images, sounds, smells, and pains may present us with feelings we would rather ignore.

There may have been moments that, in retrospect, begin to register in their full chaos and assault. It is important to remember:

1. You do not need to remember fully something that seems too fraught with emotion, particularly if you are still in a weakened state. Leave it alone until the appropriate time for engaging the memory.

2. You may want to invite a trusted friend or a spiritual director to accompany you as you recall particular moments or phases of the experience of falling ill.

3. If you feel you are ready to recall a moment in the illness that was particularly painful or wrenching, approach the recalling slowly and gently.

Compassion toward Ourselves

When we begin doing this practice of *lectio*, many of us are still vulnerable physically, psychologically, emotionally, and spiritually. So enter the process with care and compassion. As we begin to revisit those moments when we heard the physician say, "I'm sorry; the mass is malignant," or when a sudden onslaught of pain left us undefended, we encounter real fear that may have been buried or hid from our sight. We begin to pay attention to those moments when the room was spinning as we took in hard news, changing everything irrevocably. In this process we may retrieve impressions, sensory experiences, momentary glimpses that serve to guide us in living with the illness.

Isabel had been taken to an emergency room in extreme pain, and though her initial hours in the hospital were a blur, she began to recall a body memory of a hand on her forehead. Though Isabel was not sure whose hand it was, her body remembered the touch, which gave her the gift of knowing she was accompanied even in the throes of the pain. Revisiting this memory, this page of the text of her illness, proved to be a touchstone for Isabel in the long months of recovery that followed, giving her a sense that a Presence was standing with her through thick and thin. Eventually she was led to write a note to the staff of the emergency room. Not knowing to whom specifically her thanks should be directed, she decided to thank them all, for it seemed that the one person who stood with her represented the work of the community of doctors, nurses, and technicians. Isabel's reading of this moment in the text of her illness entailed recalling those embodied memories that were directly connected to the trauma of her pain and the sudden onset of her illness. As she read this experience, she began to slowly "read, mark, learn, and inwardly digest," bringing prayer to the hours in the emergency room. She let herself be honest as she uncovered her own feelings of vulnerability and fear, realizing how stunned she was, to her very core, by the pain. All of this was read and remembered.

For Isabel, the reading, this *lectio* movement, took some months. The memories were too strong and too diffuse to be digested quickly. She did the reading with her spiritual director and with a trusted friend. As Isabel read the memories of what her body went through, a deepening tenderness and reverence for her own flesh began to emerge. With time, gratitude for her body and her life started to well up, and she found herself remembering a line from a hymn: "When through the deep waters our pathways shall lie / thy grace all sufficient will be our supply." She was able to read the text of her illness honestly, without embellishment or glossing over. She discovered that in the midst of so much crushing pain and disorientation, there were glimmers of gracious Presence.

PRACTICE

Before beginning to recall the text of your illness, you may wish to invite a trusted friend, family member, or spiritual companion to accompany you. Though the meditations may be done in solitude, the reflection on those readings may release strong emotion. Having another person in whom you can confide and with whom you can reflect will give you support in prayer and in remembering. Choose someone who will not interfere with your own process of interpretation, and will also courteously allow you to enter the *lectio* process gently and at your own pace. Anyone who is living with illness is slowly discovering the new identity that comes in the aftermath of physical distress. This newly emerging identity is tender and vulnerable and needs to be entrusted to persons of wisdom, kindness, and utmost compassion.

Recalling

After I got home from my first hospitalization, I discovered that I had sore spots from being given shots that I had no memory of receiving, and I had to ask my husband what had happened. Depending on how your illness began, this may happen to you, too. Your memories may be either crystal clear or a bit hazy, and sometimes in the crush of an acute onset of illness, both the physical trauma and the pain medication may cause blank places in memory. Don't fret if there are moments—or days— you don't remember. Give your memories time to emerge.

1. As you begin the practice of *lectio*, start with the affected part of your body. If you have a chronic pulmonary disease, for example, begin by noticing your lungs, and recalling the memories associated with the onset of the disease or the initial diagnosis. Breathing gently and steadily allows your focus to rest on the affected organs, limbs, and systems. Let yourself pay attention to images, memories, and impressions that come to mind, and if something in particular keeps returning to your awareness, notice it and write it down.

2. As you enter the process of recalling, note your feelings. There may be some sadness, relief, gratitude, fear, wonder, despair. Do not judge your feelings; simply allow them to be known and to be received. If you are a person for whom writing

is an expressive outlet, you may want to write about your feelings. Others may wish to talk about them, or to paint them. The point is to acknowledge the particular text of your illness, allowing yourself the space and time to discern the layers of bodily sensation, memory, and emotion. Don't hurry; don't set a deadline. Be as slow and deliberate as necessary.

Reading a Scar

If you've had surgery, the reading of the scar may be the place to start your *lectio*. Regarding the incision lets the reality of the surgery sink in. In the case of mastectomy, the incisional site is also a site of amputation. The scar itself may be read in a variety of ways. For some, it may be a sign of loss. For others, a sign of both loss *and* life. A scar is a clear sign that something has happened, that a body has been cut into and has been altered. As an outward and visible sign, the scar may intimate both wounding and healing. If you have a surgical scar, the following suggestions for reading that flesh are one way to engage this text.

1. Choose a position that will allow you to touch the scar. If it is on your back, you may want to stand or to sit on a stool. Begin by noticing your breath. Allow yourself to inhale and exhale gently, pausing for a beat at the end of the inhalation. Breathe in this manner for several minutes, praying, "My body shall rest in hope" (Ps 16:9).

2. Gently trace the scar with your fingers. Let your fingers rest on the scar tissue as you return to the gentle breathing and praying of "My body shall rest in hope." After several minutes, continue touching the scar, and listen. Notice what emotions, associations, and memories come to you. Bless the scar tissue with a simple prayer of thanksgiving for the body's ability to grow new cells: "Thanks be to God for a body that creates new

tissue." You may want to sign the scar with a cross or perform another gesture, ritual, or prayer that is more fitting to your circumstance and body. The point is to become aware of the body's injury and its capacity to knit together.

3. In your journal, write about this experience. Allow yourself to read this text with care by writing about your impressions. If you found the meditation to be unhelpful, write that. If the touching of the scar made you uneasy, write that. Be honest and start where you are.

4. Offer a prayer in response to the reading of the scar.

Reading a Chronic Ailment

If you live with a chronic illness like diabetes or lupus or chronic fatigue syndrome, how do you begin to read its text? One way to begin is to start with a presenting physical challenge. If you are regularly administering shots of insulin, that may be the place to begin reading. If you have the troublesome symptoms of chronic fatigue syndrome, start with one symptom. Let yourself focus on this symptom, not to examine but simply to listen.

1. Following the basic pattern of getting in a comfortable physical position, breathing gently and steadily, notice your feelings toward the detail that is your beginning text. For example, how does the flesh respond to the entry of the diabetic syringe? Have you done this so long that there is a kind of familiarity or is it new enough to cause distress? Place your fingers gently on the place where you are presently administering the injections and continue to breathe gently as you pray, "My body shall rest in hope." Listen for the associations and emotions that come to you while reflecting on the dispersal of the insulin through the tiny viaducts of your body, on the minute channels that connect all of the tissues and allow the insulin to

circulate. Give thanks for those systems that allow you to live with your ailment. Bless the skin through which the needle enters, using a simple prayer of your own devising.

2. In your journal, write about the prayer and the experience of noticing your body's effective dispersal of the insulin. Remember that your body has been knit together by God. Notice whatever resistances or confusions may arise. Be honest in your responses and in your prayer. If the prayer becomes "I hate this business of injecting myself with insulin," begin there. Tell yourself and God the truth.

On the other hand, if you begin to realize that much about your flesh is marvelous, even though you live with illness, let that be the prayer. "I will thank you because I am marvelously made; your works are wonderful and I know it well" (Ps 139:14).

Further Suggestions

Your body may suggest how to begin the reading of its text. Though you may think this statement is ridiculous, sometimes the presentation of an ache or a twinge or a soreness will provide a place to begin. The important thing is to begin, and to do so without presupposing the outcome. *Lectio* with a body that suffers from illness is the beginning of an extended conversation, a befriending of your flesh that has been bruised and incised. Reading your text begins with your specific illness, with your intuition and experience indicating where to start, how to pray, what ritual to employ. Above all, allow yourself to become kindly aware of your body, not only of what has been hurt but also of what is mending, healing, and working. Notice what is already present, both sickness and health. Read the full text, not the cheap summary. Read with slow and merciful care, mindful of the divine compassion that holds you in life.

CHAPTER 6

Meditatio

~

"CHEWING THE CUD"

E sther endured a difficult surgery. She was haunted by her experience of darkness in the recovery room, a postoperative darkness that was somehow different than what she remembered from prior surgeries. Initially, Esther couldn't find words to describe the darkness, so she began to paint it. Using acrylics and paper, she worked with the dark tones of the palette—black, dark brown, navy blue, a green that was almost black. Esther discovered that in her postoperative state, the darkness had not been malevolent or forbidding, but filled with Presence. In her practice of *meditatio* (in this case accomplished through the medium of painting), she began to remember a line from the Psalms: "Darkness is not dark to you" (Ps 139:11). As she prayed, both with the paint and with the text, her interpretation of the surgery began to shift. Esther began to see the darkness as welcoming, encompassing, maternal. Her unfolding sense of the text of her body, the text of her illness, led her then to embrace another line from Psalm 139, despite her slow and halting recovery: "I will thank you, for I am marvelously made" (Ps 139:13). Although Esther's initial meditation was accomplished via the medium of paint, in time, words began to come as well. The words rang true because they were grounded by the *meditatio* with color and shape.

Esther entered the *meditatio* phase by ruminating on an image that welled up from the memory of her surgery. It's similar to the process we follow with Scripture, as we focus on a particular word, phrase, or association. This is the time when the "chewing" occurs, as we gently repeat the phrase or word that catches our attention. In the repeating we note what comes to mind in our moments of quiet concentration on the phrase. As we learned in Chapter 2, *meditatio* encourages us to ruminate, like a cow, taking the time to ingest and digest the meditation.

At this point in the process of reading the text of an illness, having recalled a particular moment in the illness or perhaps become aware of some detail of our own afflicted body, we focus on an image, sound, or bodily sensation. Choosing a particular moment of the illness, a particular experience, allows us to sit with that moment and listen for associations. Scriptural connections may occur to us, and intimations of meaning may appear. There is not a "right" way to do this. Simply pay attention to what you remember, and spend as much time in meditation as is comfortable for your body and your spirit. Your particular limitations will help you determine what is personally appropriate.

Enter *meditatio* with an open heart and spirit, remembering that *lectio divina* is a way to listen with the ears of the heart. Let the inner silence well up; listen not only with your ears, but with your eyes, your memory, and your body. Listen with your whole self. You may not have a sense that questions are being answered. Rather, this phase may be a slow unfolding of deeper layers of your experience of being physically ill. There is no need to hurry, or to try to push this meditative time to some foregone conclusion. *Meditatio* with illness allows you to notice without judging and to be present to your own body's life.

NON-VERBAL EXPRESSION

Like Esther, you may find that the process of *meditatio* requires a nonverbal means of expression. Because you're listening to what Jungian analyst and author Ann Ulanov has called "body-speech,"[12] this may *not* be the kind of listening that hears words. According to modern communication theory, most of the way we communicate with one another in face-to-face encounter is not through words, but through gesture, body language, and facial expression. The speech of your body is like that, too. In *meditatio* with your body, pay attention to what is mediated without words. The phrase "body language" is part of our everyday speech; in *meditatio* with illness remember that the body does have its own language, and that this language conveys meaning in nonverbal ways.

As you practice *meditatio,* note your awareness of how you received what you know and remember of the illness. Perhaps your intuition picked up on something before it came to your conscious perception. *Meditatio* invites you to remember ways of knowing that are not necessarily cognitive, helping you move more readily into the realm of symbol, image, impression, and intuition. For example, Caroline remembered the office visit when she received her diagnosis of a malignancy. This encounter kept coming back to her, nagging for attention. As Caroline focused on a particular interchange between herself and the doctor, she realized that the physician's body language had communicated the severity of the situation before he opened his mouth. She discovered that she had "caught" his concern at an intuitive level. But as helpful as the physician's concern was, Caroline wanted to find her own stance toward the cancer. She discovered through *meditatio* that while the physician's response was compassionate and urgent, her own true response was more pragmatic and reflective. *Meditatio* allowed her to be grateful for the physician's care, and to give herself the time to explore her own feelings and attitudes toward the malignancy. Through *meditatio* she was afforded the space and time to differentiate her own feelings, fears, and hopes. She discovered that her feelings and values were not always the same as those of her physician, her family, and her friends. This process of prayerful differentiation and discernment allowed Caroline to carefully reflect upon—and fully embrace—her treatment choices, despite the harsh side effects. She began making decisions that were informed not only by medical information, but also by a clearer sense of her own values and her own hopes. She found that *meditatio* gave her the inner space and time to "chew" on her decisions, to reflect inwardly on treatment options, and to pray about her choices. The *meditatio* began with her willingness to revisit the moment before the physician spoke, as his body language spoke a concern that his voice did not convey. Caroline's intuition caught the moment, and by returning to her intuitive perception, she was able to begin sorting out her own feelings and begin a process of discernment.

MEDITATIO AND PERSONAL BOUNDARIES

When grappling with illness, you're in a more vulnerable state, into which the reactions of others come charging. These reactions may range from supportive, helpful, and faithful to disturbing and invasive. As you try to discern your new identity within the matrix of your illness, the opportunity to listen carefully to the experience of your illness, to the internal conversations going on between mind and body and soul, allows for grounding and growing. It also allows for differentiation—for simply knowing how you feel and think and regard the life now marked by the presence of this stranger that is illness. *Meditatio* as a regular practice allows you to catch up with yourself during the assault of tests, exams, and treatment. It allows you to focus, to listen, to take the time to perceive what you may have overlooked in the midst of turmoil.

Just when you need time for quiet reflection, you're bombarded with the voices and opinions of family, friends, and even strangers. Most of the time, they don't mean any sort of harm. That makes it hard to reject inappropriate, ill-fitting opinions offered in friendship. But you can listen to your body for cues about how to respond to these opinions. You can use *meditatio* for the gentle repeated revisiting of a conversation or a letter or an e-mail in which a questionable counsel is offered, giving you the time to register your body's response to these opinions. Do your muscles tense? Does your stomach knot? Do you find yourself holding your breath? These are some ways your body may be saying very clearly that the interpretations and opinions being so freely offered are in fact very costly to your body and soul. The body that has been broken will speak in its own language if you just give it a chance.

MASSAGE THERAPY

It may be helpful to enter into massage therapy, if this is appropriate for your physical state and is supported by your doctor.
Therapeutic or healing touch can help you hear what your body
is saying as it allows the release of hidden grief or other deep
emotion. And using massage therapy to support *meditatio* can
continually ground you in the reality of the experience of your
illness, helping to screen out received interpretations of the illness that are either wrong or invasive. The prayerful practice of
massage therapy can be a form of anointing for healing, sup-
porting body and soul in living with the illness.

Should massage therapy or healing touch be a way in which
you choose to practice *meditatio*, be sure to get references for
practitioners whose training has prepared them for appropriate
care of a body that is mending. Seek references from others who
are living with illness themselves, or from your physician.

A WORD ABOUT DREAMS

One important way the text of your illness may present material for *meditatio* is through dreams. Keep a journal and pen at
your bedside. The dreams received as you live with illness may
offer a gold mine of cues. Unexamined emotions, ideas for
recuperation, creative response to limitation and trauma—all
these may be discerned by tending to your dreams.

If you have never paid attention to your dreams, this may
seem to be an odd suggestion. But remember that in Scripture
a variety of spiritual encounters transpires within dreams—
from King Solomon's request for a listening heart to Gabriel's
annunciation to Joseph in the Gospel according to Matthew.
Scriptural narrative presents us with a ready acceptance of

dreams as a means of encounter with God and as a means of discernment.

In addition, the language of your dreams is deeply connected to the language of your body. Both tend to be symbolic, redolent with image and impression. A dream may also encourage you to pay attention to symptoms that you're trying to ignore, or point to an aspect of living with your illness that needs to be addressed. *Meditatio* with dream imagery can help you enter the world of the dream, listening for its wisdom in the context of your illness.

If you haven't paid much attention to your dreams, you may at first remember only the feeling tone of the dream. Don't despair. That's a good place to begin. Write down your impressions, even though they may be vague or diffuse. This tending of the dream will help establish a practice of listening to your dreams.

ACUTE ILLNESS

Acute onset of illness jolts you from your pattern of living, radically changing your life in a matter of hours or minutes. Often the emergency room of a hospital is the space in which the illness is initially diagnosed and treated, sometimes followed by surgery or a period of time in an intensive care unit. These are highly charged environments—so much is happening as you're thrust into the care of physicians, nurses, and technicians. In those moments, your identity is quickly dismantled. Your perception of yourself as a self-sufficient, independent person is radically altered by the sheer physical necessity of being handled by other human beings. The intensity of this time, numbed by pain medications and perhaps even unconsciousness, all may combine to create a montage of impressions.

Sally suddenly became very ill at home with a burst appendix. Later she found herself remembering bits and pieces of her experience in the emergency room. At first, Sally recalled only vague images, but later, as she began to heal from a surgery and an extended hospital stay due to infection, she found that she remembered more than she initially realized. Some memories, razor sharp, appeared as Sally began to recover her strength. In revisiting those memories during *meditatio*, she discovered that despite the atmosphere of crisis, on some level she had felt very still. The phrase from Psalm 46:1, "God is our refuge and strength, a very present help in trouble," came to her in prayer. Sally later reported that it felt as if her awareness were resting deep beneath the surface of a clear lake. On the surface of that lake, there was bustling activity; at the deeper level, there was stillness.

In some cases of acute illness, this *meditatio* phase of the process will allow a person to consciously register events that were rapid and intense. Charles had a gracious breakthrough as he focused on a particular moment in the emergency room following his heart attack. Charles found that the *meditatio* phase called him to focus on the face of a particular nurse who was among those attending him. As he remembered her face in the circle of faces over his gurney, he sensed that she was praying very intentionally as she did her job. Her face helped him put a face on the compassion he encountered and gave Charles a new sense of Christ's presence in suffering. As he returned his inner gaze to her face during prayer, he sensed that God's maternal presence was very near and merciful. While Charles still struggles with a weakened heart, this maternal image has led him to reflect. He has begun to reflect on death as a birth to eternal life. The face of the nurse has become an icon for him, a window through which he glimpses a mothering presence that will not let him go, that will accompany him even in the process of dying.

PRACTICE

Meditatio on Becoming Ill

Materials needed: journal, pen

1. In a comfortable position, perhaps sitting or lying on a bed with knees supported (a bolster or a rolled-up towel under the knees), begin by paying attention to your breath. Inhale and exhale gently, drawing your breath down into your belly. As you breathe, notice if your muscles are tense. Direct your breath to those areas. Let yourself simply breathe for several minutes, and allow your body to relax.

2. Recall the onset of your illness. This may be a moment of sudden disruption and pain, or a moment in a doctor's office when you received test results, or even a phone conversation in which your physician reported your diagnosis. Choose a moment that you associate with realizing that you were ill.

As you remember this time, notice your own physical responses. Pay attention to your breath, to the tensing of muscles, to any body language that may help you reflect on the experience. Is your solar plexus knotting up? Are you holding your breath? Are certain muscle groups responding? Is your heart beating faster?

3. Notice the feelings that come with your recollection. Remember that you may have a variety of feelings, from anxiety to anger to worry to puzzlement. Let yourself register your own responses in that moment. You may want to repeat a line from a Psalm as you recall these moments, for example: "God is

our refuge and strength, a very present help in trouble" (Ps 46:1) or "Out of the depths have I called to you, O LORD" (Ps 130:1).

4. Having noticed your feelings and perceptions, make note of them in your journal. As you return to these recalled moments, using *meditatio*, keep a record of what you remember.

The next chapter will offer suggestions for *oratio*, the prayer created from the *meditatio* experience.

Meditatio with a Dream

Materials needed: journal, pen

1. Begin, as in the previous exercise, with the first step, relaxing and letting yourself become aware of your breath. Recall the dream that you need to reflect upon. Let yourself notice color and sound, as well as your own feelings, as you recall the dream. Upon what part of the dream does your attention focus?

2. As you pay attention to this particular aspect of the dream, notice your feelings, questions, and concerns, and write them in your journal. You may want to draw an image from the dream, or to paint the image.

3. If this is a dream that continues to ask for attention, allow yourself to return to *meditatio*.

4. Keep a record of the associations that come to you during *meditatio*.

5. Form a prayer that speaks of this experience, perhaps something as simple as "Dear God, I need your guidance and wisdom as I seek to understand."

CHAPTER 7

Oratio

~

CREATING PRAYER

D uring my recuperation from pancreatitis, as I lay in bed without the energy to concentrate or even to intercede for myself, I encountered grace and mercy in a way that's all but forgotten in our culture. I began to let go—forced by the sheer fact that my body could hardly move—and received a sense of the many threads of intercessory prayer holding me up. A friend suggested that I relax into that weaving of prayers, trusting that others were offering intercessions on my behalf. It was an unnerving and new experience, but resting in the prayers of others was the *oratio* I practiced for many months. A singularly transforming and humbling experience, this *oratio* of receiving the mercy of others' prayers led me to perceive that even though much of my time was spent by myself at home, I was not alone. It was also an occasion of deepening trust in the grace and mercy of intercession and in God's presence throughout the experience.

For me, this was a true experience of the *oratio* phase of *lectio divina,* as my prayer sprang organically from my time of *meditatio,* expressing the deepest yearnings of my heart. When you're physically weakened, perhaps by treatment or by the illness itself, *oratio* may be a form of receiving the intercessions of others. In the words of Benedictine sister Joan Chittister, "To pray when we cannot is to let God be our prayer."[13] This may be an opportunity to let the intercessions of others be the tensile webbing that supports and upholds during prayer. Rather than creating prayer, you can simply *be* prayer, receiving the intercessions of others and letting go.

For all of us, the stirrings that come to our attention during *meditatio* seek expression, not always in words, but sometimes in other ways. You may feel a desire to draw or to paint their prayers, or discover that working in clay allows you to bring the prayer into an outward and visible form. Perhaps movement such as gentle yoga practice or simple dance may give form to your prayer. The main thing is to find an expressive form that is genuine and appropriate to your physical condition—it could be something as simple as a gesture of your hands cupped and open. As you walk through your illness, *oratio* is a moment of truth, as you allow your fears, heartaches, and weakness to spill forth. Sometimes, desperate silence may be your very deepest prayer.

PRAYER AND CHRONICITY

If you suffer from a chronic illness, marked by a pattern of repeated tests and doctor visits, your *oratio* may form naturally

out of the pattern of your days. Tom, who was enduring chemotherapy treatment, began to regard the chemicals administered
to him as sacramental. He approached each intravenous treatment as a form of communion, praying that the Christ "in
[whom] all things hold together" (Col. 1:17) would guide the
elements of the chemotherapy to restore him to health. He
came to the treatments repeating the words from his tradition
for the distribution of consecrated bread: "The body of Christ,
the bread of heaven." For him, this *oratio* hallowed the ritual of
receiving the treatment and named his deepest desire for healing of body, mind, and spirit.

Juliana, having to make radical dietary adjustments following two surgeries, discovered that the act of feeding herself
appropriately seven times a day took the form of a daily office.
She meditated deeply on the need to eat, and on her depend-
ence on the food to keep going, recognizing that eating inti-
mated her mortality. If Juliana didn't eat, sooner or later she
would die; if she didn't eat properly, the consequences would be
painful. So Juliana allowed the feeding of herself, even when she
was not hungry, to become a form of communion. She discovered that her *oratio*, a yearning that the food be absorbed and
become her new flesh, opened up profound dimensions of the
sacramental life. The required feeding, which had at first felt
like a prison, began to be an occasion for receiving the love of
God, embodied through the requisite foods. One day this
Scripture came to her: "You ... are in me and I am in you" (John
17:21), beginning a new cycle of *lectio, meditatio,* and *oratio.*

Like Tom and Juliana, let your prayer originate from the
point of encounter of the actual details of your experience of
illness, rather than from some idealized or imagined state. After
letting the moment of *meditatio* open the door of association,
memory, and imagination, allow the movement to *oratio* to

invite you to make the prayer authentically incarnate. Don't flinch from the fact of your physical limitation or from the sometimes difficult passages of being ill. Your prayer is true when it is intimately connected to the visceral experience of your suffering. Your *oratio* that has its origin in this truthful reflection may startle you with its graphic suggestion, blowing apart saccharine assumptions about cure. It may subvert the interpretations your family and friends give to your illness, or their handy recommendations for how to get well. This *oratio* is grounded in *your* lived truth. It's grounded in your body, which is constantly communicating the stress and the resilience, the capacity and the emptiness of your experience.

PRAYING WITH LIMITATIONS

One way that the *oratio* opens the door to truth is that it often helps you become aware of the limits within which your illness calls you to live. For example, if your new diagnosis requires a high-protein, low-fat, low-sugar diet, you may find yourself in open rebellion. The prohibition of certain favorite foods may be very difficult, and may even involve some real grief and stress, especially if your partner doesn't share your dietary restrictions. But if you take this restriction to a form of *oratio*, your inner movements of sadness, distress, longing, and desire about the new regimen could be formed as prayer in any number of expressions. The essential aspect is that the *meditatio*, when done honestly, allows you to know what is roiling around inside as you attempt to put on a new identity—in this case, a new identity defined in part by a dietary regimen. Then the prayer you offer as your *oratio* is grounded in lived experience that's connected to your real life.

HUMOR

Carmen, who was undergoing radiation, meditated on the experience of the machinery that administered her treatments. She would reflect on the positioning of her body, on the noises that were something of a ritual, on the sensations of lying on the X-ray gurney. Carmen found herself humming a hymn tune, which she didn't even like, as her *oratio* flowed forth in the form of this tune. She suddenly realized that the words to the tune were "Shine, Jesus, shine." With this realization, she laughed out loud. Of Latino origin, she decided to privately name the X-ray machine "Jesusito" (a term of endearment for Jesus in Spanish). Carmen's *oratio* was marked by humor and tenderness, and by a growing awareness that even the machinery of the X-ray machine was held together by the bonds of divine love.

Like Carmen, we can all bring a sense of humor to the *oratio* phase, as we can with many ways of prayer. In this case, the lightness of humor may lead us to see unexpected metaphor and double entendre in our own prayer, leading us to the paradoxical moment when truth telling leads to laughter.

CREATIVITY

Giving form to prayer assumes that it needs to be birthed, to be brought forth so that we may know more fully what the prayer tells us about ourselves and about our ongoing relationship with God. Whether the prayer is simply lying and breathing quietly, or making a hand gesture, or moving the whole body, or painting a picture, *oratio* invites creative participation in the mutual disclosure that is true prayer. We reveal more of our true selves to God, who graciously meets us and intimates divine presence and guidance in a variety of ways—some of them curiously oblique and obscure.

Surprisingly, through *oratio* you may begin to discover creativity in the midst of your illness. If you've listened deeply to your experience of being ill, and to Scripture, you begin to hear the conversation that unfolds, as Scripture informs your illness and your illness illumines the Scripture. In small ways, you may begin to notice that you're slowly being renewed. Literally, cell by cell, your body is being sustained as the subatomic particles that make up your cells are held together in love and mercy. The cells themselves come together to knit new flesh and to remove waste, to transport oxygen and nutrients.

Allowing yourself to notice, through *meditatio*, the myriad functions that your body is carrying out without your conscious intervention may awaken your wonder even when you're struggling to deal with discomfort. Adriana began to see her circulatory system as rivers of life, channels and tributaries of real blood coursing through her body. Her prayer initially took the form of sketches. She first went to a standard encyclopedia and looked up the anatomical map of the circulatory system. Then Adriana began to sketch in shades of red, drawing impressions of the circulating life within her hands, her feet, her trunk. In the drawing, she began to repeat the phrase "river of your delights" from Psalm 36:8.

This extended *oratio* led her to begin to reflect on the ecology of her own body, on the need to supply appropriate food, rest, water, and exercise so that the rivers within her might flow well. The creative nature of her prayer started with her reflection on her own body, her own veins, arteries, capillaries. In the meeting of that reflection with Scripture, something new and creative began to unfold, and is still unfolding. She began to think of the ecological concerns that she has for the world, and her own contributions to the clean-up efforts for rivers in her area. Adriana still lives with the ailment that led to the process of using *lectio divina* with her body. She has not experienced cure, but she has experienced a form of healing in that her own relationship to her body and to her life has made a creative and holy shift.

PRACTICE

Oratio with Gesture

1. Find a comfortable position, perhaps sitting with good support or lying down. Begin by paying attention to your breath. Gently inhale and exhale, letting your breath move more deeply into your trunk and abdomen with each repetition. Go slowly and do not hurry. Let your body rest in the breath. As the breath establishes a rhythm, notice if your muscles are tense in any particular area. You may find that you may need to adjust your position slightly in order to relax. Be mindful of your own particular physical needs and stresses.

2. Begin repeating "In You I live and move and have my being" as you breathe. (You could make a variation on this line by shortening it to "In You I live.") After praying this for a while, focus your attention on whatever part of your body is afflicted. If you suffer from a systemic disorder, simply envision your whole body or that system. Let your imagination guide you.

3. Notice as you pray (now moving into *meditatio*) what feelings, images, associations are brought to your attention as you tend this part of your body.

4. Cup your hands in prayer (if you are lying down, just let your hands remain by your sides and cup them in place). Let

the gesture of your hands be the prayer. If you cannot move your hands, return your attention to your breath and let the breath be the bodily gesture of receptivity.

As you let the gesture be the prayer, give thanks for the hands and for the breath that are signs of the prayer. If possible, bring your hands together over your heart and gently bow your head as a sign of thanking God and of receiving the mercy of the prayer.

Oratio with Written Form

Materials needed: journal and pen

1. Repeat steps 1–3 of the prior exercise.

2. Having noticed the feelings, images, and associations, ask in prayer for a word from the Word. You may do this with a simple phrase: "Please give me a word." Listen for a response. Write down the word or words that you receive. For example, you might receive the word *flesh*. Write that down.

3. Create a prayer using the word you have been given. Using "flesh," you might write: "My flesh is failing me; I need God's help." Another possibility would be: "I give thanks for the flesh that is healing." Create a response that is truly yours, springing from the reality of your body's illness and from your honest inner state. Remember that spiritual practice always begins where you are, not where you think you ought to be.

4. Return to this exercise as needed, creating prayers that are as honest and to the point as possible.

Oratio with Color

Materials needed: paper and crayons, colored pencils, or color markers

1. Repeat steps 1–3 as in the exercise *Oratio* with Gesture.

2. As you move into *meditatio,* discern if a particular color seems to be associated with your prayer. Of course, you might notice that a variety of colors are connected to the prayer.

Pay attention to the prayer welling up within you, taking the form of color. You might notice a color within your own body as you meditate, or you might notice a color that predominates in a memory or an image. Notice the color and let yourself pay attention to shading and shape. Are there feelings that come with this particular color? Is it a color you enjoy, dislike, don't particularly care about one way or the other?

3. Using the paper and the pencils, markers, and/or crayons, color the paper with the color that has been present in your *meditatio.* You're not making a sketch or drawing, and you're also not being graded on your art. Simply apply the color to the paper, and let that be your prayer. Let yourself concentrate on the color as it appears on the paper. If a shape comes forth, fine. If not, that's fine too.

Once you've applied the color to the paper, put the paper on the wall or in your journal—someplace where you will see it regularly. The color itself may lead to unfolding layers of prayer. Recall the woman whose postsurgical experience led her to paint in dark colors, not knowing what that was about. Color can be a means for us to encounter a deeper prayer that is held in our bodies.

Oratio with Clay

Materials needed: easily pliable clay or Playdough, journal and pen

1. Repeat steps 1–3 as in the previous exercise *Oratio* with Gesture.

2. After being in *meditatio,* take some clay and allow yourself to simply knead the clay, letting your hands come to know its texture. Offering your prayer, work the clay. You do not need to be "making" a particular shape or item. The interchange between your hands and the medium of clay is the starting point. As you work the clay, you may notice that some shape begins to form without your imposing a particular idea. Again, this is not about creating a perfect piece of art. You are allowing a prayer to form in the clay. As you work with the clay, you may notice feelings or memories that arise. You may want to note these in your journal.

Working with clay sometimes brings us startlingly honest prayers about our bodies. The handling of clay reminds us of our own earthly substance infused with life. It is also possible that the prayer is initially nonverbal and that the process of handling the clay is itself all that needs to happen in the moment. Again, don't hurry and don't worry about a fixed outcome. Instead, allow your hands to do the deep listening. Approach this *oratio* with patience. If you have never prayed in this way, it may seem completely and utterly strange. It also might provoke some anxiety. Remember that there is no goal involved; working the clay as a form of *oratio* is a way to listen to the experience of being ill, and to bring that experience into prayer.

CHAPTER 8

Reading the Text of a Chronic or Progressive Illness

∾

THE RECURRING TEXT

I f you live with chronic illness, the text of your body has many recurring motifs. It is almost like reading a long poem with a recurrent chorus. Office visits, X rays or other diagnostic tests, the drawing of blood, and the ingestion of medication all become part of the ongoing narrative of your illness, and adjusting to these routines can seem overwhelming. As with the formation of any new habit, you need to direct a degree of conscious intent toward making appointments, taking medicines at the appropriate times, remembering to adjust your diet to your ailment. It may be difficult at first to regard any of the changes prayerfully. You may feel distraught, bewildered, sad, or simply lost amid the details. The new learning curve can be fairly steep, as you absorb and integrate the implications of your physical condition.

That's precisely where the *lectio divina* process with this text of chronic or progressive illness may begin. Allowing yourself to read the variety of your responses to the major changes in diet, exercise, body image, and lifestyle will allow your prayer to be honest and faithful. Perhaps your reading of the text of your chronic illness will lead you to the psalms of lament, and perhaps you will echo the cries of "How long, O LORD?" (Ps 13:1). With chronic or progressive illness, cure is not likely, but healing is. Your body may be afflicted with any number of symptoms, yet genuine, undefended prayer will lead you to the healing that comes with telling the truth in love.

The fact of living with chronic illness is a lifelong reality that invites regular *lectio, meditatio* and *oratio*. Millions of people live with some sort of chronic or progressive illness, from diabetes to lupus, from emphysema to scleroderma. Often they're given injurious counsel—under the guise of prayer—that fails to take into account the reality of chronic illness and implies that the person who is afflicted remains unhealed because of insufficient faith.

In fact, the person living with chronic or progressive illness is often learning real lessons about life and death that our culture desperately needs to remember. Chronic illness may of necessity remove us from the frenetic and acquisitive pace of our society and force us to come to terms with the distorted values of a consumer culture, leading us to life-giving decisions within the context of our limitations. Living daily with illness teaches us lessons about compassion, suffering, mortality, and hope. *Lectio divina* with chronic or progressive illness can help uncover lessons through our diminished bodies.

After my second hospitalization, I read an article that gave me some real insight for living with chronic illness. The author, a woman rabbi living with lupus, noted that she discovered that she had needed to "come out" to herself, to recognize the fact that she indeed was suffering from a progressive illness, and that she needed to adjust the way she lived.[14] She observed, "I didn't realize the extent to which I had been leading, for so long, a double life—a sick person posturing as healthy. I had pushed myself for so long—my whole adult life. So there were always two people operating in my one body, and one of them was a liar."

When I read this article, I began to become aware of the ways in which my tendency to push myself aggravated the weakness of my body. I was denying my illness, rather than accepting the fact of my forever-changed body. And though forming habits of rest, nutrition, exercise, and prayer that honestly supported my recovering body and soul was essential, it could only happen if I was ready to acknowledge the fact of the illness. The first step was to let myself accept the truth in love, thereby letting go of behaviors that looked like "passing" for a person who had no affliction. I had to "come out" to myself.

Rabbi Schnur suggested creating new norms within the parameters of an illness, norms grounded in "coming out" to ourselves about living with chronic or progressive illness. She concluded the article with "So I'm trying to spend these months becoming 'visible' to myself as a chronically ill person." In other words, she invited the reader to see the fact of illness honestly and faithfully. Stepping out of the little illusions we can create for ourselves may be quite a challenge, but failing to do so may make us sicker in body and soul.

Rabbi Schnur's words offered a way of living with chronic illness that didn't put me in the role of victim. "Coming out," as she put it, meant spending far less energy pretending I was "just fine, thank you," and giving more attention to ways to support my body with its real limitations. Her words gave me permission to tell myself the truth about how I felt physically and spiritually. Over time, I began to form new habits as the balance necessary for life with an injured organ emerged.

But after the initial stock-taking, from time to time, that balance changes and needs to be reexamined. That's where the process of *lectio divina* with the body comes in, leading us to greater honesty about our physical limitations.

LIVING WITH LIMITATIONS

Living with chronic or progressive illness inevitably means living with limitations—but *all* humans live with limitations. When our bodies are healthy and functioning well, though, it's easy to forget that each of us is mortal and defined by a variety of limitations, from language, to culture, to family traditions. Each limitation helps define who we are while ruling out other possibilities. While as human beings we may have the freedom to make choices, those choices are always made within limits. Living with chronic or progressive disease brings this reality into focus in ways that are both excruciating and illuminating.

Laura, on being diagnosed with multiple sclerosis, felt as if the limitation of her disease taught her about the other limitations of her life. She was initially enraged by the multiple sclerosis, but over time, the rage moved to anger and then began to abate. Laura recognized that she was not the only person in the world who was suffering, and the limitations of the disease began to open her more deeply to compassion toward others. A former executive, very efficient and organized, she discovered that there was still a possibility for life, even within the limitations of her own ailment. Her spiritual director suggested that she go to a local grotto at a Roman Catholic seminary and light a candle as a sign of her prayer. When she went to do this, she was astounded by all of the other candles that were burning, an outward and visible sign of the suffering of others. Laura began to be delivered from the strange (but prevalent) notion that God had personally selected her for the suffering. She realized that there were many different kinds of suffering, and that each person's pain had its own nuance and grief.

When Laura joined a support group, she also found that each person had a different experience of the multiple sclerosis. She discovered the limitation of assuming that her experience of the disease was the same as everyone else's, and she also discovered the danger of generalizing from her experience. She discovered that reading the text of her own progressive illness might give her ways to connect with other persons living with MS, but did not necessarily mean she knew what their experience would be. All of this proved to be humbling, in ways that were sometimes uncomfortable. Yet Laura discovered that through the regular confrontation with her own physical limitations, she began to understand her own behaviors. She noticed that she had been controlling toward others and not particularly respectful of their abilities and disabilities. As she became more practiced at reading the text of her illness, she became more able to express both her sadness at the deterioration of her body and the gratitude for her ability to function fairly well for the moment.

MEDICATIONS

The text of chronic illness inevitably includes a kitchen counter or a bathroom cabinet or a bedside table filled with bottles of prescribed medications for the ailment. The bottles themselves are often invested with layers of meaning. For some, they're conveyers of support and life; for others, they're the bars of a prison cell. Inevitably they seem to form an important part of the text of an illness, and their presence invites regular meditation and reflection.

Other forms of administering medications, such as syringes for those with diabetes and morphine patches for those living with chronic pain, can also have the same degree of import. For those who live with chronic lung disease, the portable oxygen machines used at home and in the car become invested with symbol and meaning as well as pragmatic function. If you live with chronic or progressive illness, pay attention to the medications and to the machinery or technology that you regularly encounter. Take the opportunity to read this part of living with illness.

TRIPS TO THE PHARMACY

The presence of medications in any form also leads to the regular practice of going to a pharmacy. Purchasing the medication entails the necessary interaction with one's insurance carrier (if one has insurance) to pay for the medications. These pages of the text of living with illness are often full of tension, frustration, and confusion. The fact is that many people who live with illness do not have adequate medical coverage, so obtaining the requisite medications entails financial distress, hard choices, and real difficulty in balancing the needs of a household. In this case, the text of the illness very clearly involves a household, and also directs us to the larger body of society. All of this is appropriate for *lectio divina*.

Earl, who had insurance coverage, went monthly to the local pharmacy for his prescription. His physician, for medical reasons, changed the medication, but the new drug was not on the list of those covered by his insurance. But the problem wasn't overwhelming: he had enough money in the bank to cover the $250 monthly check for the medicines. However, as he waited in line, practicing *lectio* in the moment, he listened to the ongoing conversation at the counter. Earl realized how many of his cosufferers did not have the financial means to do so. Returning home later in the day, he had the time to reflect in quiet and stillness. During *meditatio* he kept remembering one older man who was trying to purchase medicine for his wife but didn't have enough money. The reflection on this moment led Earl into an *oratio* in the form of intercession for the elderly man and his wife, and for the personnel at the pharmacy who are confronted daily with these kinds of situations. The *oratio* led him into the larger community of those who live with chronic illness, and began to change his self-pity into an awareness of his own privilege. It also began to lead him into a desire to address the lack of health care for so many people.

NUTRITION

Inevitably, living with chronic or progressive illness leads to attention to food and nutrition. Those who suffer from heart disease, diabetes, kidney disease, and a variety of digestive disorders quickly learn that they need to feed themselves with care. Often our first notice about nutrition comes in the form of a printed handout the doctor gives us, with lists of prohibited and suggested foods. Inevitably, favorite foods are on the prohibited list. This disruption in something as primal as what we eat can be very difficult indeed.

Most of us are unaware of the feelings and associations that we have about food until we're forced to make some changes in the way we eat. As we adjust to a new dietary regime, we may experience rebellion, grief, sadness. It can also be overwhelming at first if prior knowledge of nutrition is nil. This part of the text of a chronic or progressive illness is ever present. In some cases, not following the appropriate plan for nutrition can lead to life-threatening consequences.

It may be helpful to meet with a dietician or nutritionist to help sort out the details of your particular plan. I found it imperative to find a good nutritionist for guidance about what—and how—to eat. I was fortunate to find one who understood the sadness of abstaining from a favored cuisine. As I adapted to five or six small meals a day, rather than the three large meals I was accustomed to, I had to confront my own unease with being set apart by my nutritional needs.

As we practice *lectio divina* with food and nutrition, we're brought face to face with mortality in a surprising way. We're confronted with the fact that ingesting the wrong foods could hurt our bodies and provoke severe medical consequences. We're aware that if we don't eat, we'll die.

At the heart of this reflection, we're dwelling on the mystery of the Eucharist. Just as Christ feeds us in and through the sacrament of the bread and the wine during Holy Communion, so too we are fed every time we eat. The challenge is to discern the opportunities for communion at every meal, even when our favorite foods are not permitted. Real adjusting to a new dietary regimen makes this discernment difficult at first. The adjusting can be a means for becoming intentional and prayerful about our eating, and for deepening gratitude for the food on our tables.

Upon being diagnosed with type two diabetes, Bud found himself very depressed. The list of foods he could not have seemed to have no end, while those he could eat weren't ones he'd have readily chosen. Bud's nutritionist helped him reflect on his memories associated with food. The fried foods he loved dearly—french fries, fried pies, fried chicken—were all associated with his maternal grandmother, who would cook them for him when he came to visit her. Giving those foods up felt like sundering a tie to his grandmother.

He discovered that his first task was to let himself be honest, even though it felt embarrassing, about the fact that these fried foods were dear to him. It was not just a matter of the flavor and texture, though of course that was part of the attraction, but the fact that these foods echoed happy moments from his childhood. He found that as he did *meditatio* he uncovered sadness over the loss of this link to his grandmother. His nutritionist and his spiritual director helped him recognize the tenderness of that relationship, and how deeply he cherished it. Once in a while, he has a homemade french fry as a form of communion.

Bud also had to embrace a kind of eating that was healthy for his body, but felt alien to his established way of eating. Fruits and vegetables, small portions, far less sugar than he had formerly enjoyed—this was but a beginning. Again the metaphor and reality of communion was helpful to him. He realized that more than anything, he wanted to support his own health so that he might live to enjoy his own grandchildren. Appropriate nutrition began to have a communal dimension. He realized he needed to eat in a way that supported his health not only for his own well-being, but for that of his family as well. The way in which he related to his diabetic regimen was gradually transformed as he perceived the requisite food as a form of prayer.

Eventually, after several years, his prayerful approach to food also made him aware of hunger in his own community. He began to become active in the hunger program in his church and to take a particular interest in helping others like himself who had been diagnosed with diabetes. By allowing himself to discern the layers of meaning in the somewhat disconcerting sadness about losing his favorite foods, he began a repeated practice of *lectio divina,* which led to ever-enlarging circles of compassion and awareness. He still struggles with some of the dietary restrictions and misses some of the foods he had to give up. Bud also has discovered some new foods that he enjoys that he had never eaten before.

His prayerful encounter with his dietary needs as a diabetic began when he decided to be honest about his sadness about not eating the foods linked to his grandmother. This first step was very disconcerting. After all, a grown man should be beyond such feelings! His decision to tell himself the truth, even if it felt embarrassing, allowed him to move into a continuing *lectio,* engaging life with diabetes in a different way.

PRACTICE

Lectio Divina with Regular Medical Tests

1. Find a comfortable position, either sitting or lying. Bring your attention to your breath. Notice the inhalation and exhalation, the gentle rush of air through nostrils and airways. Breathe in and out, letting the breath move deeper into your abdomen.

2. Recall one of your regular medical tests. This could be blood work, or CAT scans, or any regular diagnostic procedure. As you recall this experience, what do you notice? Are there physical reactions that register? What do you notice about your feelings or emotions? Be honest.

3. Having recalled this particular procedure, focus on one aspect of it. For example if you are having a CAT scan every three months, you might focus on your thoughts and feelings as the scan is occurring, or on how your body responds to the

experience of the procedure. Let your awareness rest on this particular aspect of the testing. As you focus, you might pray, "Your servant listens" or "You are with me always" or whatever phrase fits your circumstances.

4. As you proceed with the *meditatio,* notice the feelings, thoughts, associations, Scriptures, songs, and memories that might register as you reflect. You may want to write these in your journal.

5. Create a prayer that gathers up the experience of *meditatio.* Perhaps this prayer will accompany you the next time that you have this diagnostic procedure.

Lectio Divina with Medicines

If your ailment requires the regular ingestion of prescribed medications, these have become an intimate part of your existence. This practice is intended to help you become aware of the medicines consciously and to bring them into prayer.

1. As in the previous exercise, begin by finding a comfortable position and by breathing gently.

2. Recall your medicines and their containers. Picture them in your imagination as they are arranged on a countertop, or at your bedside, or in a cabinet. Notice the variety of containers. As you reflect on the medication prescribed for your illness, what feelings do you notice? Your feelings may be contradictory, but pay attention to them anyway.

3. Bring one of these feelings into intentional prayer. Keep it simple: "Dear God, I resent taking this medicine." Or: "Thank you, Jesus, for the medicine that keeps me going." Be mindful about both the medicine and about how you relate to it.

4. Begin reflecting on others who take the same medication. Pray for them.

5. Recall the researchers whose efforts resulted in the medicine. Pray for them.

6. Recall the pharmacist who filled the prescription. Pray for her/him.

7. Recall those who need the medication and cannot afford it. Pray for them.

8. Finally, note in your journal what you might have noticed or discovered in your meditation. If this needs to take a creative form in paint or gesture or movement, allow that to happen. If you have received an insight about a prayer to accompany the ingestion of your own medication, write it in your journal and use it as you take your medicines.

Lectio Divina with Dietary Regime

1. If your chronic or progressive ailment requires that you follow a nutritional regimen, you've probably been given written guidelines to follow. Start with them. Sitting or lying comfortably, with the written instructions for your diet in your lap, place your hands on the pages. Begin breathing gently.

2. Recall your feelings and thoughts as you began to adapt to the regimen required by your physical condition. When you were given suggestions about which foods to eat, about how often to eat, about portion size, what were your responses? Recall the foods from which you need to abstain. The list may be long or short. Among those forbidden foods, is there one in particular that you miss?

3. Focus on this particular food. What memories, associations, and feelings are associated with it? Do you notice sadness or a sense of loss? Are you irritated or angry about having to give this food up? Allow yourself to notice the feelings and memories without judging them.

4. Choose one memory or association that is linked to this particular food. What do you notice? Write this in your journal.

5. Create a prayer that addresses your ties to this particular food. The form of the prayer will be as particular as the food and the associations. You might want to begin with a phrase such as "Gracious God who feeds us . . ." or "Loving Spirit whose bounty blesses us with food." Let the prayer include the variety of feelings that have come to you. Let yourself be honest and to the point.

Conclude the prayer by giving thanks for the food that you may eat and for the fact that you are alive to eat it.

CHAPTER 9

The Voice in the Whirlwind

∼

JOB AND HIS FRIENDS

A t the end of the book of Job, after Job has listened to his friends' various theological explanations for his misfortunes, he rejects all of them. Afflicted in every way, he won't allow his suffering to be explained by facile answers. He has lost possessions, children, health, prestige. Job asks—demands— a direct conversation with God. He asks for God rather than an interpretation of God. He seeks Presence, not theory. This is a risky move, and the only one that allows him to move beyond the pat explanations of his horrendous loss and illness.

When the divine voice speaks to him from the whirlwind, it doesn't bring an explanation from God. Rather, the Voice,

speaking from the whirlwind of his life in chaos, from the tor-
nadic vortex of his suffering, asks, "Where were you when I laid
the foundation of the earth?" (Job 38:4). Job says in response to
the Voice , "I had heard of you by the hearing of the ear, but now
my eye sees you" (Job 42:5). Hearsay has become encounter. Job
has met with the divine presence, here depicted as a whirlwind.
This is not the still, small voice of Elijah's encounter, but a voice
speaking from the elemental creative forces of the cosmos, the
Holy One who is Trinity, who brings forth the elements and
creates all that is, redeems all that is, sanctifies all that is.

The author Stephen Mitchell notes that Job's vision is rooted
in the things of this world.[15] Job comes to terms with being a creature and with being mortal. He is given a vision of himself within
the context of the whole created order; he surrenders to becoming what he already is: part of a whole that comes from God and
returns to God. In Mitchell's translation, Job says, "Therefore I
will be quiet, comforted that I am dust."[16] Coming to terms with
being a creature has brought comfort in the midst of the affliction. Job's encounter with the Voice reframes everything.

As you learn to read the text of your illness, you'll be aware of
those explanations and answers that may be handed to us with
the best of intentions, explanations and answers that are a poor
substitute for the Voice that speaks from the whirlwind of your
illness. As you practice *lectio divina* with your body, your illness,
and your life, you begin to discern the presence of the God in
whom you live and move and have your being. You discover that
the explanations are not God, nor are easy answers God. You
discover in a discomforting and honest way that there is no
substitute for listening with the ear of the heart for the voice of
the Christ, in whom all things hold together. In time, you may
even begin to think of your illness not only as a source of disruption and despair, but as a source of understanding what

really matters, what life really looks like. You move into the ten-sion of living with a "both/and" orientation, rather than an "either/or." You know the presence of Christ intimately through your suffering and illness. As you're formed by that presence of the Incarnate Word, you move beyond explanation to encounter.

Illness may give us the raw experience that leads to encounter. One early morning several years ago as I was driving my son to school, I heard a program about cancer on the radio. A group of cancer patients was being interviewed about how they had managed to live with the surgery, the chemotherapy, the radiation. They spoke of the help of friends, family, doctors, nurses, support groups. Then one woman said, "I know this sounds crazy. I still don't have any hair. Yet the fact is that cancer has been a good teacher. If I hadn't had the cancer, I doubt I would realize the extent to which I was not living the life I hoped to live. The cancer has been—in a peculiar way—a friend."

Illness makes us stop, often literally. The fact of our mortal-ity looms large: One day we will die. Our illness may or may not give us a clue about how that dying will occur, but it reminds us that our bodies—fragile and resilient—will wear out. As our very flesh wears down, we find that there is something within us that does not die. We wake up to the life of God within human life. Within the context of the illness, the holy Presence abides, often hidden or obscured, yet abiding. One facet of the many facets of meaning of Jesus' crucifixion is that God is with us in suffering. In the vision of Jesus on the cross, we perceive the divine presence intimately, excruciatingly, with us in our pain, our grief, our loss, our dying.

We also defend ourselves against this knowing in a variety of ways. Perhaps we think it is a gift too good for us to embrace, a gift too intimate—that God in Christ knows and experiences our travail from the inside out. The Word was made flesh and continues to dwell among and within us through the power of the Holy Spirit. That indwelling is without restriction, without inhibition. God in Christ is there in the diminishing tissue, in the cells struggling to receive nutrients, in the bones being X-rayed. In Christ God reveals the indissoluble tie with all that is created, a bond that is not sundered by illness or by death.

OTHERWISE

When I was recovering from my first hospitalization in 1995, a friend gave me a copy of *Otherwise*, a book of poems by Jane Kenyon. An accomplished poet who struggled with depression, Jane Kenyon was diagnosed with leukemia and died fifteen months later, in April 1995. The poem from which this collection takes its name invites us to another fruit of *lectio divina* with the body—gratitude.

> I got out of bed
> on two strong legs.
> It might have been
> otherwise. I ate
> cereal, sweet
> milk, ripe, flawless
> peach. It might
> have been otherwise.
> I took the dog uphill
> to the birch wood.
> All morning I did
> the work I love.
>
> At noon I lay down
> with my mate. It might

have been otherwise.
We ate dinner together
at a table with silver
candlesticks. It might
have been otherwise.
I slept in a bed
in a room with paintings
on the walls, and
planned another day
just like this day.
But one day, I know,
it will be otherwise.[17]

When I first read this poem, it named for me a reality that
the attack of acute pancreatitis had forced home. I was at home
recovering, but it could have been otherwise. I was able to walk
to the bathroom, but it could have been otherwise. I could pat
my sleeping cat's head, but it could have been otherwise. A kind
of gratitude that I had not fully known began to emerge.

You might have the same kind of experience. Once you move
through the initial shock at discovering you're not as you once
were, that your body may be changed forever, the diminishment
that illness brings may also offer the gift of knowing what could
be otherwise. A deepening gratitude, and something that looks
like surprise and wonder, may begin to enter, even though your
affliction is severe. You no longer take for granted the simplest
acts and the most basic necessities. You're less likely to mind-
lessly gobble the warm peach and the sweet milk. Your "otherwise awareness" wakes you up to the gift of being in the present.
A piercing sense of life's beauty and grief may release both hope
and wistfulness. The growing appreciation of the shortness of
your life (even if you live to be one hundred) helps you reorder

your priorities. You begin to know that there will be a day when you're not here to welcome the first north wind of autumn or to eat the tiny new asparagus from the back garden. Paradoxically, you come to know this life as gift and treasure as you learn to let it go. Like Job, you recognize that you'll become dust, yet you acknowledge that you're dust fashioned by the hands of the living God.

As you read the text of your illness, you may discover inchoate desires for meaning, for connection, for being fruitful, for loving God, your neighbor, and yourself. You may discover, in short, that there is no place where God is not.

"BEING SPIRITUAL"

One of the odd ways we think about spirituality is to imagine that you can only be spiritual if you're always happy, peaceful, prosperous, and healthy. This could not be further from the proclamation of the Incarnation. In the words of Benedictine sister Joan Chittister, "If we are not spiritual where we are and as we are, we are not spiritual at all."[18] Practicing *lectio divina* with illness is a way of living out an incarnational spirituality that refuses to avert its eyes from a body that is in the throes of disease. At the heart of this practice is the conviction that the Christ indwells all that is, even bodies that are torn or emaciated or paralyzed.

Saint Benedict's Rule invites you to enter a school for beginners. In a way, your illness itself is a school for beginners. Learning to live with it means starting over, living with real limitations, and telling yourself the truth about what you can and cannot do, eat, experience. "Always we begin again" is Benedictine counsel.[19]

When illness comes and you start over, you're often given new perceptions of time. On the one hand, the sense that chronological time is short may weigh you down, and with a terminal diagnosis the sense of time ticking away can be overwhelming. On the other hand, illness can be a radical clarifier. The fact of a weakened body can make you aware of the shortness of your life. Time may seem both short and full. You may find yourself aware of *kairos* moments.

Kairos is the Greek word used by the New Testament writers to speak of a moment full of presence and meaning, a time when something is being brought to fruition and purpose. The phrases "in the fullness of time" and "the appointed time" have traditionally been used to translate *kairos*. Almost anyone who is seeking to live faithfully will experience moments of *kairos* time. Illness, because it leads us to begin again, and reminds us of our creaturely nature, leads us to *kairos* awareness. Moments we might have overlooked are noticed. Encounters that would have been forgotten are remembered and prayed about.

Kelly, who was in dialysis treatment for end-stage kidney disease, found herself acutely aware of her granddaughter's growth. At two years old, the granddaughter was learning new words almost daily, and practicing her newfound independence with spirit. The grandmother, knowing full well that she would not live to see the granddaughter grow to adolescence, found herself paying careful attention to the changes that she might have overlooked before her illness became severe.

Illness teaches us to approach time differently. Within the context of illness, we may discover what Abraham Heschel called "holiness in time."[20] In the midst of tests, blood work, CAT scans, hospitalizations, physical therapy, there may be an unexpected inbreaking of grace and mercy, of beauty too exquisite for words, of tenderness and friendship that stir us with sighs too deep for words.

Beginning again because of illness precludes a perfect outcome. But a perfect outcome, thank God, is not the point. What is? The point is to listen ever more deeply for the living Trinity within and through the circumstance of your illness. Beginning again allows you to listen to your body and your illness, knowing that the Voice may speak even in the whirlwind. And even though you're dust, you're beloved dust, the work of God's hands. Reading the text, listening with the ears of your heart, letting yourself tend your body and your experience of disease invites you, like Job, to refuse explanations and demand God's presence and seek God's face—perhaps where you least expected.

Appendix:
Some Frequently Asked
Questions

~

T he following are some questions that are often asked when I teach this material.

What if I feel like my whole body is an illness?
Start with that perception. Begin with the practice of having someone outline your body on a piece of butcher paper. Then perhaps you can use color to help you visualize something that is systemic and hard to pinpoint. Another possibility would be to focus your reflection on a locus of pain or discomfort, and to offer some gesture of kindness and thanksgiving to that area that is hurting.

Is it possible to do lectio *with depression?*
The focus of this text has primarily been physical illness. However, members of my classes have told me that it has been helpful with mental illness as well. For example, if you need to take medications for depression, the meditation on pages 101–102 could be used for those medications. *Lectio* could be applied as you notice the onset of depression and the feelings (or lack thereof) that accompany that onset.

Can adolescents use this process?
In the groups I have worked with there have been some younger people who were very open to the process. They may have less familiarity with Scripture, and may need some help in that regard. The important issue is that the person desire to try this practice.

Can this be used with a group?
I believe that the practices could be done in a group setting, as long as a few norms were established. I would suggest borrowing a norm of "no cross talk" from 12 step recovery process. Most of us have already had too much help and need the space and time to make our own discernments. I would also suggest confidentiality, meaning that anything shared within group time is not spoken about outside the group. The exception would be if the speaker invited others to speak to him/her directly outside the group.

I would suggest that if this is done in a group, that an hour and a half is needed for the process. However, those who are participating and who know the limitations of their bodies will be the best guides for establishing length of time. I strongly suggest that beginning and ending time be observed with care, in consideration of physical limitation.

It has also been helpful to have a diverse group. In other words, my experience has not been with groups whose members were all living with the same kind of illness. While that could definitely be one kind of group that could use these practices, it is also possible to have a group whose members have different ailments.

Suggestions for Further Reading

~

BENEDICTINE SPIRITUALITY AND *LECTIO DIVINA*

Canham, Elizabeth J. *Heart Whispers: Benedictine Wisdom for Today*. Nashville: Upper Room Books, 1999. This is a grounded, common-sense, and accessible exploration of essential aspects of Benedictine spirituality.

Chittister, Joan. *Wisdom Distilled from the Daily*. San Francisco: HarperSanFrancisco, 1991. A lively and clear explanation of Benedictine spirituality, this book is very helpful for understanding the Benedictine tradition.

DeWaal, Esther. *Seeking God.* Collegeville, MN: Liturgical Press, 1984. As a member of the Church of England, DeWaal brings an Anglican perspective to Benedictine spirituality. She also offers insights about the Rule's application to families.

Hall, Thelma. *Too Deep for Words: Rediscovering* Lectio Divina. New York/Mahwah, NJ: Paulist Press, 1998. A clear exposition of *lectio divina,* with many suggestions for practice with Scripture.

McQuiston, John. *Always We Begin Again: The Benedictine Way of Living.* Harrisburg, PA.: Morehouse, 1996. Written by a layman, this book is a series of brief meditations on aspects of Benedict's Rule.

Smith, Martin. *The Word Is Very Near You.* Cambridge, MA: Cowley, 1989. Practical and concrete, this text gives clear instruction about the practice of *lectio divina.* The author, an Episcopal priest, uses anecdotes and exercises to convey his points.

Vest, Norvene. *No Moment Too Small.* Boston: Cowley, 1994. An Episcopal laywoman, Vest focuses poetically on the silence that undergirds *lectio* and the Rule.

POETRY

Howe, Marie. *What the Living Do.* New York: W. W. Norton, 1998.

Kenyon, Jane. *Otherwise.* St. Paul, Minn.: Graywolf Press, 1996.

Mukand, Jon, ed. *Articulations: The Body and Illness in Poetry.* Iowa City: University of Iowa Press, 1994.

Sewell, Marilyn, ed. *Cries of the Spirit.* Boston: Beacon Press, 1991.

Endnotes

~

1. Joan Borysenko, *Minding the Body, Mending the Mind* (New York: Bantam, 1987). The phrase "New Age Fundamentalism" comes from a workshop that Joan Borysenko offered at Kanuga Conference Center during the Spiritual Formation Conference of April 2002.

2. Timothy Fry, O.S.B., *The Rule of St. Benedict in English* (Collegeville, MN: Liturgical Press, 1982), 95–96.

3. Eileen Egan, "Polar Opposites? Remembering the Kindred Spirits of Dorothy Day and Mother Teresa," *Catholic Peace Voice* (Fall 1997), 3.

4. Joan Chittister, *Wisdom Distilled from the Daily* (San Francisco: HarperSanFrancisco, 1991), 2.

5. Hymn #516, "Come Down O Love Divine," v. 3, *Church Hymnal* 1982 (New York: Church Hymnal Corporation, 1982).

6. See, for example, Hans Urs von Balthasar, ed., *The Scandal of the Incarnation: Irenaeus Against the Heresies* (San Francisco: Ignatius Press, 1990).

7. Collect for Proper 28, Book of Common Prayer (New York: Church Hymnal Corporation, 1979), 236.

8. Thomas Merton, *The Sign of Jonas* (Garden City, NJ: Image Books, 1956), 351–352.

9. *The Rule of St. Benedict*, Prologue:1, 15.

10. Book of Common Prayer (New York: Church Hymnal Corporation, 1979), 794–795.

11. Invitatory, Morning Prayer, Book of Common Prayer, 80.

12. Ann Ulanov, *Attacked by Poison Ivy: A Psychological Understanding* (York Beach, ME: Nicolas-Hays, 2001), 25.

13. Chittister, 32.

14. Rabbi Susan Schnur, "Is Our Suffering Transformative?" *Lillith* (Winter 1996): 12–13.

15. Stephen Mitchell, *The Book of Job* (San Francisco: North Point Press, 1979), xxvii.

16. Mitchell, 88.

17. "Otherwise," from Jane Kenyon, *Otherwise* (St. Paul, MN: Graywolf Press, 1996), 214.

18. Chittister, 2.

19. *St. Benedict's Prayer Book for Beginners* (York, England: Ampleforth Abbey Press, 1993), 14. Also The Rule of St. Benedict 18:23, 73:8.

20. Abraham Joshua Heschel, *The Sabbath* (New York: Noonday Press, 1951) p. 10.

CPSIA information can be obtained
at www.ICGtesting.com
Printed in the USA
LVOW03s0236080318
569084LV00001B/22/P